50
Days
to
Pentecost

50
Days
to
Pentecost

Available from
Church Resource Distributors
Phone (417) 831-7000

CONTENTS

INTRODUCTION

God poured out His Holy Spirit on the Day of Pentecost, and the Church was born!

The Book of Acts can be outlined in three simple divisions. In chapter 1, Jesus went up. In chapter 2, the Holy Spirit came down. In chapters 3 through 28, the people went out. Jesus went up ... the Holy Spirit came down ... the people went out.

After receiving the Holy Spirit, the first Christians went out into the world and became His witnesses by proving in their daily lives what Jesus had taught them. And the world has never been the same! In Acts 17:6, some of the Jews called the Christians "these that have turned the world upside down."

Jesus promised we would receive power when the Holy Spirit comes upon us. The word *power* simply means "ability." He will give us whatever ability we need to obey our Lord's commands. Because a prominent aspect of the Holy Spirit's work is signs and wonders, many people limit the ministry of the Spirit to what we might call the "supernatural" when, in fact, He also helps us in the "natural" areas of our lives. Sometimes the divinely given "ability" we need is forgiveness toward someone who has wronged us when we don't naturally have enough love and mercy to do so.

If I could summarize what being Pentecostal means in only one word, it would be "dependent". Because we believe the divine activity of the Holy Spirit is as real and present today as it was in the Book of Acts, we depend on the Holy Spirit in virtually every area of our Christian lives. The blessed Helper is always present. The Holy Spirit guides, motivates, brings assurance and, in essence, enables us to obey our Lord's commands and live as He has ordained. "His divine power has granted to us everything pertaining to life and godliness ..." (2 Peter 1:3, NASV). As you read the Book of Acts with your family, Bible study group or prayer group, ask the Holy Spirit to teach you to depend on Him in every aspect of your life.

In 1989 the *40 Days with Jesus* Bible reading, prayer and evangelism program began in one church. The following year, 11 churches participated. The next year, more than 30. Soon hundreds of churches were participating each year. In 1993 the *50 Days to Pentecost* program began, taking people through the Book of Acts on a journey with the first Christians.

Many marvelous testimonies of God's intervention were given as people spent regular time in the Word, in prayer, and sharing Christ. Many saw non-Christian family members and friends receive Christ. During one *50 Days to Pentecost* program, a pastor's wife was miraculously healed in a prayer circle as church members joined with her in believing God as they studied the Book of Acts together.

The Holy Spirit was outpoured at Pentecost 2,000 years ago. But we need His continual fresh inpouring in our personal lives today. Just as He showed His power among the first Christians in the Book of Acts, the Holy Spirit is still moving in the midst of His people.

This updated *50 Days to Pentecost* takes families and congregations through the Book of Acts, as well as key passages from the Epistles. It also provides questions for families or small groups to discuss as they apply biblical truth to everyday living. The Scriptures are taken from a new, simplified translation of the New Testament that is especially designed for reading aloud and is easily understood by youth and children.

As you read through this study, the same Holy Spirit who

inspired Luke to write the Book of Acts will be present with you to make the words and lives of the first Christians speak to your life. The work of the Holy Spirit that took place in and through the apostles and the Early Church is still going on today.

God's Word is not just truth from yesterday; it is truth for today!

—Randy Hurst

WEEK 1

WAITING FOR THE PROMISE

Theophilus, the first time I wrote to you, I told you about all the things Jesus did and taught until the day He was taken up to heaven. He was taken up after He gave commands to the apostles He had chosen. The Holy Spirit told Him the commands to give them.

Jesus showed himself to these apostles and gave them many proofs that He was alive after His suffering.

He did this by appearing to them during a time of forty days and speaking about the Kingdom of God.

He met with all of them and commanded them not to leave Jerusalem, but to wait for the Father's promise.

He said, "You heard me speak about this. John baptized with water, but in a few days you will be baptized with the Holy Spirit."

So when they came together they asked Him, "Lord, will you bring the Kingdom to Israel again at this time?"

He said to them, "You are not allowed to know these times the Father has decided by His own authority. But you will receive power when the Holy Spirit comes to you, and you will tell people about Me in Jerusalem, in all of Judea and Samaria, and even in the farthest places of the earth."

After He said all these things, He was taken up to heaven while they watched and a cloud came over Him and they could not see Him any longer.

They looked up to heaven as Jesus went, and two men in white clothes stood beside them.

They said, "You men of Galilee, why do you stand here and look up to heaven? This Jesus who was taken up to heaven from you will come again in the same way that you saw Him go into heaven."

Then the disciples returned to Jerusalem from the Mount of Olives, that is about a half-mile trip from Jerusalem.

When they came into Jerusalem, they went to the room in the top part of the house where they were staying. Peter, John, James, Andrew, Philip, Thomas, Bartholomew, Matthew, James the son of Alphaeus, Simon the Zealot, and Judas the son of James were all there.

All of them continued to pray together frequently, and the women and Mary, Jesus' mother, and His brothers were also there with them.

On one of those days Peter stood among the brothers (there were about one hundred and twenty people who came together) and said, "Brothers, the Word of God had to become true. It was what the Holy Spirit spoke long ago through David's mouth about Judas, who became a guide for the people who took Jesus. Judas was one of our group, and he shared this work with us. (Judas bought a field with the reward he received because of the evil thing he did. He fell and died in this field. His body broke open and his insides poured out. Everyone who lived in Jerusalem heard about the field, and so in their language it was named 'Hakeldama.' It means 'Field of blood.') It is written in the book of Psalms, 'Let his house become empty, do not let anyone live there,' and, 'Let another man take his place in our work.' So we must choose one of the men who has been with us all the time when the Lord Jesus was among us, from the time of John's baptism until the day He was taken from us. This man must become a witness with us about Jesus' resurrection."

They chose two men. One of these men was Joseph, who was

also named Barsabbas (he was also known as Justus), and the other man was Matthias.

They prayed, "Lord, you know the hearts of all people. Show us which one of these two men is the man You have chosen to work in this service as an apostle instead of Judas, who left to go to the place where he belongs."

They used lots to decide, and Matthias was chosen. So he was added to the group of the eleven apostles.

Acts 1:1-26

God's people need the power of the Holy Spirit to take His message and do His works. Paul wrote about this to the Romans:

"I will not even try to speak about anything except what Christ did through me to cause the Gentiles to obey God. He did this by the things I said, by the things I did, by the power of miracles and wonders, and through the power of the Holy Spirit."

Romans 15:18-19

DISCUSSION SUGGESTIONS:

1. What did Jesus say the Holy Spirit would give to His followers and what was the purpose of this gift?

2. The disciples asked the Lord to show them exactly who should replace Judas. Does God have specific plans for each of our lives? (Read Psalm 139:13-16)

THE HOLY SPIRIT OUTPOURED

The followers were all together in one place when the Day of Pentecost came.

A sound came suddenly from heaven like a very strong wind blowing, and it filled all the house where they sat. They saw things that were like tongues of fire that separated themselves from each other, and the tongues of fire came and sat on each one of them.

All of them were filled with the Holy Spirit and started to speak in other languages, when the Spirit caused them to be able to do this.

Now there were Jews living in Jerusalem. They were religious people from every nation in the world.

The crowd of people came together when they heard this. They were confused because each person heard them speak in his own language.

They were surprised and full of wonder and said, "Aren't these people who are speaking from Galilee? Then why does each one of us hear them speaking our own languages that are spoken in the places where we were born? There are Parthians, Medes, Elamites, people from Mesopotamia, Judea, Cappadocia, Pontus, Asia, Phrygia, Pamphylia, Egypt, and places in Libya, near Cyrene, and visitors from Rome, (some people who are Jews and also those people who became believers of the Jewish religion), and also Cretans and Arabians. We hear them speak in our own languages about the great things God does!"

All of them continued to be surprised and were not able to

understand. They said to each other, "What does this mean?" But others laughed at them and said, "They drank too much wine!"

But Peter stood with the eleven apostles and spoke to the crowd in a loud voice, "You who are Jews and all of you who live in Jerusalem, listen to my words and know this. These people did not drink too much wine like you thought they did. It is only nine o'clock in the morning. But this is what Joel the prophet spoke about: 'I will pour out My Spirit on all people in the last days, and your sons and daughters will prophesy,' says God. 'Your young men will see visions and your old men will dream dreams. I will pour out My Spirit on my servants, both men and women, and they will prophesy. I will let wonders happen in the sky above, and miracles on the earth below. There will be blood, fire and much smoke. The sun will be made dark and the moon will be changed to blood before the great day of the Lord comes. Everyone who calls on the name of the Lord will be saved."

Peter said, "Men of Israel, hear these words. Jesus from Nazareth was a man whose authority from God was proved to you by great things that He did, wonders, and miracles. You know God did these things among you through Jesus. Jesus was given to you because God knew long ago that this was His plan. You hanged Him on the cross and killed Him, with the help of evil men. But God brought Him back to life and ended the pain of death, because it was not possible for death to have control over Him. David said about Him, 'I saw the Lord always in front of me. He is at my right side, and I will not be troubled. So my heart was happy and I rejoiced. My body also will live in hope, because you will not leave my soul and let it be in Hell or let your Holy One be destroyed in the grave. You showed me the ways of life, and Your presence will fill me with joy.' Brothers, I can tell you and be certain that our father, David, died and was buried, and his grave is still here now. He was a prophet and he knew

God had promised him with an oath that one of his descendants would be on his throne. He knew what was going to happen later, and he spoke about the resurrection of the Christ and that He was not left in Hell and His body was not destroyed in the grave. God brought this Jesus back to life, and all of us saw it happen. He has been made very great and taken up to the right hand of God. He has received the promise of the Holy Spirit from the Father and He has poured out these things that you see and hear now. David did not go up to heaven, but he said, 'God said to my Lord, "Sit at my right side until I make your enemies the place for your feet to rest."' So let all of Israel know for sure that God has made this Jesus, whom you crucified, both Lord and Christ."

When they heard this they were greatly troubled, deep in their hearts. They said to Peter and the other apostles, "Brothers, what should we do?"

Peter said to them, "Every one of you must repent, and be baptized in the name of Jesus Christ, so your sins can be forgiven, and you will receive a gift. This gift is the Holy Spirit. This promise is for you, for your children, and for everyone who is far away. It is for all the people that the Lord our God will ask to come to Him."

Peter told the crowd seriously about Jesus with many other words, and he gave them advice and said, "Be saved from this evil generation."

Those who accepted his message were baptized and three thousand people were added to their group that day. They continued to listen to the teaching of the apostles frequently. They continued to talk and be friends with each other, and to eat and pray together.

Everyone was full of wonder, and the apostles did many wonders and miracles. All the believers were together and they shared with each other everything they owned. They began to sell the things they owned and gave them to everyone who needed them.

They continued to meet together in the temple every day. They ate at each other's homes and they shared their food together, and their hearts were humble and full of joy. They praised God and all the people respected them. Every day the Lord added to their group the people who were saved.

Acts 2:1-47

The Holy Spirit taught the early believers that great strength and joy could come to them from their unity with each other. Paul wrote about this to the Corinthians:

> *"There should not be any division in the body. All the parts should care for each other in the same way. All the parts suffer together if one part suffers, or all the parts have joy together if one part is honored. You are the body of Christ, and each one of you is a part of it."*

1 Corinthians 12:25-27

DISCUSSION SUGGESTIONS:

1. Peter told the people if they would repent and be baptized they would receive a gift. What was that gift?

2. How did the lives of the new believers change and what does the Bible say the Holy Spirit will bring to people? (Read Romans 5:5)

SPEAKING THE TRUTH

Peter and John went to the temple at three o'clock in the afternoon. This was the time for prayer.

There was a man who had been crippled since he was born. Every day they put him at the temple's door named 'Beautiful', to ask for money from people who went into the temple. He asked Peter and John for money when he saw that they were going into the temple.

Peter looked straight at him, along with John, and said, "Look at us." He looked at them and expected to receive something from them.

But Peter said, "I do not have silver and gold, but I will give you what I have. Get up and walk in the name of Jesus Christ of Nazareth."

Then Peter took his right hand and lifted the crippled man up. His feet and his leg bones received strength immediately. He jumped up and stood on his feet and started to walk. He went with them into the temple, and he walked and jumped and praised God. All the people saw him walk, and praised God, and they knew he was the man who sat and asked for money at the temple's door that is named 'Beautiful.' They were full of wonder and great surprise because of what had happened to him.

While the man who had been healed held on to Peter and John, all the people ran to them in the place named 'Solomon's Porch' and they were full of great wonder.

When he saw this, Peter said to the people, "You men of Israel, why are you surprised because of this man? Why do you look at us like that? Do you think we made him able to walk by our own power and goodness? The God of Abraham, Isaac, and Jacob, the God of our fathers, has given glory to His servant Jesus. You gave Jesus to the authorities and rejected Him in the presence of Pilate, when Pilate wanted to let Him go. But you did not accept the Holy and Righteous One, and you asked Pilate to give you a killer. You killed the Giver of life whom God brought back to life from death, and we are witnesses of this.

This man, whom you see and know, was made strong because of faith in Jesus. Perfect health was given to this man in the presence of all of you, because of faith in Jesus. Now brothers, I know you did this because you didn't know who Jesus really was, just like your rulers did. But God announced long ago through the mouths of all the prophets that His Christ should suffer, and He has caused these things to become true in this way.

So repent and turn to God, so your sins can be taken away. Then times of rest and blessing will also come from the presence of the Lord, and He will send the Christ who was chosen long ago for you. This is Jesus. He must remain in heaven until the time when all things will be made right again.

God spoke this through the mouths of His holy prophets who lived long ago. Moses said, 'The Lord God will give you a prophet like me from among your brothers. You must listen to everything He tells you. Every person who will not listen to that prophet will be completely separated from the people and destroyed.' Samuel and all the prophets who came later and spoke, also told about these days. You are the sons of the prophets and of the promise that God made to your fathers. He said to Abraham, 'All the families of the earth will be blessed through your descendants.'

God brought forth His Servant and sent Him to you first, to bless you and to cause every one of you to turn away from your evil ways."

Acts 3:1-26

The power of the Holy Spirit was given to help us speak and live in a way that will make people listen to the good news about Jesus Christ. Paul wrote about this to the Thessalonians:

"Our gospel did not come to you in words only, but also with power and the Holy Spirit, and with great assurance of its truth. You know what kind of men we were when we lived among you. We did this because of you."

1 Thessalonians 1:5

DISCUSSION SUGGESTIONS:

1. When the crippled man was healed, how did Peter respond to the crowd's admiration?

2. What does Peter's example teach us? (Read 1 Peter 3:15)

OBEY GOD OR MAN?

The priests and the captain of the temple guards and the Sadducees came to Peter and John while they spoke to the people. They were greatly troubled because Peter and John taught the people, and preached that people are brought back to life from death through Jesus. They took Peter and John and put them in prison until the next day, because it was already evening.

But many of the people who heard the message believed it and the number of people who believed increased to five thousand.

Their rulers, leaders, and teachers of the Law met together in Jerusalem the next day, and Annas, the high priest, was there. Caiaphas, John, Alexander, and all the men who were from the family line of the high priest were also there.

They put Peter and John in front of them and asked them, "By what power or by what name did you do this?"

Then Peter, who was filled with the Holy Spirit, said to them, "You leaders and rulers of the people, if we are being asked to explain today about a good thing that was done for a crippled man, and about how this man was healed, then all of you and all the people of Israel should know that it is by the name of Jesus Christ from Nazareth, whom you crucified and whom God brought back to life from death, that this man stands here in front of you and is healed completely. Jesus is the 'stone that you, the builders, did not accept. But He has become the chief corner stone.' There is no one else who can give us salvation. And there is no other name under heaven given to men, by which we must be saved."

When they saw the courage of Peter and John and understood that they were men who were not educated and not trained, they were full of wonder, and then they remembered that these men had been with Jesus.

They did not have anything to say against Peter and John when they saw the man who was healed standing there with them. They talked to each other after they had ordered Peter and John to go out of the council.

They said, "What will we do to these men? They have done a great miracle and everyone who lives in Jerusalem knows about it. We cannot say it isn't true, but it must not be talked about among any more people. Let's order them not to speak any more to any person in this name."

So they called them and ordered them not to speak or teach at all in the name of Jesus.

But Peter and John answered them, "Decide for yourselves whether God believes it is right for us to listen to you and obey you, or to listen to Him and obey Him. We must speak about the things we saw and heard."

They let them go after they had given them more threats. They could not find any reason to punish them because all the people praised God for what had happened, because the man who was healed was more than forty years old.

Peter and John went to their group after they were freed, and they told them everything the chief priests and leaders said to them. When the group heard this, they joined their voices together and prayed to God.

They said, "Lord, You are the One who made the heaven, the earth and the sea, and all the things that are in them. You caused the Holy Spirit to speak through the mouth of our father David, Your servant, and said, 'Why did the nations become violently angry, and the people think useless things? The kings of the earth stood, and the rulers came together, against the Lord and against His Christ.' It is true that Herod and Pontius Pilate met together with the Gentiles and with the people of Israel, to go against Your holy servant Jesus, whom You anointed. They did what You had already decided long ago by Your power and purpose would happen. Now Lord, hear their threats against us, and give Your servants courage to speak Your message as You reach out Your hand to heal people, and as miracles and wonders happen through the name of Your holy servant Jesus."

The place where they had come to meet together was shaken after they prayed. All of them were filled with the Holy Spirit, and they spoke the message of God with courage.

Acts 4:1-31

Telling others about Jesus may not always be easy, but the Bible shows us that the Holy Spirit will always give us what we need when the time comes. Paul wrote about this to the Thessalonians:

"We suffered and were shamed at Philippi, as you know, but God helped us and gave us the courage to speak to you about His gospel even though there was much opposition."

1 Thessalonians 2:2

DISCUSSION SUGGESTIONS:

1. The Jewish leaders knew Peter and John were not educated
or trained and they were amazed at the disciples' courage. What did
the leaders then remember about Peter and John?

2. When Peter and John told believers about the threats, what
did they all pray for and what happened? What can this mean for
us? (Read Psalm 138:3)

SHARING EVERYTHING

All of the believers were united in their hearts and souls. They shared everything they had, and no one said anything belonged only to him.

With great power the apostles told people that they knew that the Lord Jesus was brought back to life from death. Great blessing from God was with all of them.

There was no one among them who was needy. This was because everyone who owned land and houses sold them and brought the money from the things they sold, and gave it to the apostles. Then it was given to the people, when any of them needed it.

Joseph, whom the apostles gave the name Barnabas, (that means, "Son of Encouragement") was a Levite who was born in Cyprus. He had a field, and he sold it. Then he brought the money and gave it to the apostles.

There was a man named Ananias and his wife, Sapphira, who sold some of the land they owned. He kept part of the money, and his wife also knew about this. He brought part of the money and gave it to the apostles.

But Peter said, "Ananias, why has Satan filled your heart and caused you to lie to the Holy Spirit, and to keep part of the money from the land you sold? Didn't the land belong to you before it was sold, and didn't you have control over the money after the land was sold? Why did you think of this in your heart? You did not lie to men. You lied to God."

Ananias fell down and died after he heard those words, and great fear came to everyone who heard this. The young men got up and put a cloth around his body and carried him out to bury him.

His wife came in about three hours later, and she did not know what had happened. Peter asked her, "Tell me, did you sell the land for this price?" She said, "Yes, that was the price."

But Peter said to her, "Why did both of you agree together to test the Spirit of the Lord? The men who buried your husband will also carry you out."

Immediately she fell down near his feet and died. Then the young men came in and found her dead, and they carried her out and buried her next to her husband. Great fear came to everyone in the church and also to all the people who heard about these things.

The apostles did many miracles and wonders among the people, and all of the believers met together often in Solomon's Porch. But none of the other people had the courage to come there and be with them, even though the people respected them very much. But more and more men and women believed in the Lord, and they were added to their group.

They even carried out the people who were sick into the streets and put them on beds, so at least the shadow from Peter's body could be over some of them when he came there.

Crowds of people from the cities around Jerusalem also came together to bring sick people and people who were greatly troubled by evil spirits. Every one of them was healed.

Acts 4:32-5:16

The reasons behind our giving to God and the way we feel about giving to Him are as important as what we give Him. Paul wrote about this to the Corinthians:

"But I tell you, the person who plants only a little will also receive only a little, and the person who plants much will also receive much. Each person should give what he has decided in his heart, and not unwillingly, and not because he is forced to, because God loves people who have joy when they give."

2 Corinthians 9:6-7

Discussion Suggestions:

1. Who told Ananias he must give the money from his land to the church?

2. What can this teach us about God's attitude toward our giving to Him? (Read Exodus 25:2)

SUFFERING AND SERVING

But the high priest and all the people who were with him, who were from the Sadducees' group, were filled with jealousy, and they took the apostles and put them in a public prison.

But an angel from the Lord opened the prison doors during the night and brought them out.

The angel said, "Go and stand in the temple and speak to the people all of the message about this Life."

So after they heard this, the apostles went into the temple very early in the morning and taught the people.

But when the high priest and the people who were with him came, they called the council leaders and the leaders of the people of Israel together, and they sent some of them to the prison to bring the apostles to them.

But the men who went did not find them in the prison.

They returned and said, "The prison building was locked when we went there, and the guards stood at the doors. But when we opened the doors we did not find any person inside."

The captain of the temple and the chief priests were very troubled when they heard those words.

They were troubled about what would happen because of this.

Someone came and told them, "The men you put in prison are standing in the temple and teaching the people."

Then the captain and the law officers went and brought the apostles. But they did it without any violence, because they were afraid the people would stone them.

They put the apostles in front of the council when they brought them in.

The high priest said, "We strongly ordered you not to teach in this name. You have filled Jerusalem with your teaching, and you want to make us guilty of this man's blood."

But Peter and the other apostles answered and said, "We must obey God rather than men. The God of our fathers brought Jesus back to life, whom you hanged on a tree and killed. God made Him great and took Him up to be a ruler, and a Savior at His right hand, to give the people of Israel the opportunity to repent, and to forgive their sins. We and the Holy Spirit are witnesses of these things. This is the Holy Spirit God gives to those who obey Him."

The leaders were very angry when they heard these things, and they wanted to kill the apostles.

But there was a Pharisee named Gamaliel. He was a teacher of the Law. All the people respected him, and he was also a Pharisee in the council. He stood up and ordered them to take the apostles outside for a short time.

Then he said to them, "Men of Israel, think carefully about what you are planning to do to these men. Some time ago, there was a man named Theudas, who told people he was an important person, and about four hundred men joined him. But he was killed, and all the men who followed him went to many different places, and everything they were doing became nothing. Judas from Galilee came after that, at the time when the people were being counted, and he took some people to follow after him. But he died also and all the people who followed him went to many different places. So I tell you, stay away from these apostles, and leave them alone. This is because the things they are doing will fail if they are people's plans and ideas. But if they are God's plans you will not be able to stop them, because then you will just find yourselves fighting against God."

They agreed with him, and they called the apostles to come to them. They ordered the apostles not to speak in the name of Jesus, and they freed them after they beat them.

So the apostles left the council. They had great joy because they were worthy to suffer shame because of Jesus' name.

They did not stop teaching and preaching that Jesus was the Christ. They taught this in the temple and in houses every day.

Acts 5:17-42

The Holy Spirit can help us have the same kind of commitment and joy the apostles had in serving Jesus. Paul wrote about the reason the apostles continued to tell about Jesus, no matter what trials they faced:

"Christ's love controls us, because we are convinced that one man died for all people, and so, all people have died. He died for all people, so the people who live should not live for themselves any longer, but for Him, who died and who was brought back to life again for them."

2 Corinthians 5:13-15

Discussion Suggestions:

1. What did the angel from the Lord tell Peter and John to do as soon as he let them out of prison? What did Peter and John do as soon as the angel let them out of prison?

2. Whom did Gamaliel tell the Jewish leaders they might be fighting if they killed the apostles? What assurance does this give us? (Read Exodus 14:14 & Deuteronomy 3:22)

WISDOM FROM THE SPIRIT

The number of followers increased during that time, and the Greek Jews started to complain against the Hebrews. They did this because their widows were not given enough food when it was given out to people each day.

The twelve apostles called the crowd of followers to come to them and said, "It is not good for us to stop preaching and teaching God's message so we can serve food at the tables. So brothers, choose seven men in your group whom everyone knows are full of the Spirit and wisdom. We will give this responsibility to them. But we will continue to give our attention to praying and preaching the message."

This suggestion pleased all of them.

So they chose Stephen, a man full of faith and full of the Holy Spirit, Philip, Prochorus, Nicanor, Timon, Parmenas, and Nicolas, a man from Antioch, who had become a Jew.

They brought these men to the apostles, who prayed for them and then laid their hands on them.

More and more people heard the message of God, and the number of followers increased greatly in Jerusalem, and many priests also accepted this faith.

Stephen was full of God's blessing and power, and he did great wonders and miracles among the people.

But there were some people from the synagogue named the Synagogue of the Freedmen. They were both Cyrenians and

Alexandrians. There were also people from Cilicia and Asia.

These people all came and argued with Stephen. But they were not able to do anything against what Stephen spoke, because he spoke with wisdom, and it came from the Spirit. So they brought in some men secretly to say, "We heard him speak evil words against Moses and against God."

They caused trouble among the people, and the teachers of the Law and the leaders came and took Stephen.

They brought him to the council, and they brought people there who lied and said, "This man never stops speaking against the Law and the Holy Place. We heard him say that this Jesus of Nazareth will destroy this place and change the traditions that Moses gave to us."

All the people who were in the council looked carefully at Stephen, and saw that his face was like an angel's face.

Acts 6:1-15

Nothing that happens can take the freedom and joy of the Holy Spirit from those who are His. Paul wrote about this to the Corinthians:

"The Lord is the Spirit, and there is freedom where the Spirit of the Lord is. But all of us look at the Lord's glory with uncovered faces, just like looking in a mirror, and this glory, that comes from the Lord, who is the Spirit, changes us so we will become like Him from glory to glory."

2 Corinthians 3:17-18

DISCUSSION SUGGESTIONS:

1. When the disciples chose Stephen to help the people, what two things were said about him?

2. The Bible says if we have the Holy Spirit, there is something we can know. What is it? (Read 1 John 3:24)

GOD'S FAR-REACHING PLAN

The high priest said, "Are these things true?"

Stephen said, "Brothers and fathers, listen to me. The God of glory appeared to our father Abraham when he was in Mesopotamia, before he lived in Haran. God said to him, 'Leave your country and your family, and come into the country that I will show you.'

Then Abraham came out from the land of Chaldea, and lived in Haran. Then his father died and God brought him into this country, where you live now. God gave him nothing, not even a foot of the ground.

But God promised He would give the land to Abraham and that he and his descendants who lived later would own it, even though he did not have any children at that time.

God spoke and said that Abraham's children would live in a strange country, and they would be like servants, and people would do evil things to them for four hundred years. God said, 'I will judge the nation where they will be servants, and they will come out from there and serve Me in this place.' God gave Abraham the covenant of circumcision, and so Abraham became the father of Isaac, and he circumcised him on the eighth day. Isaac became the father of Jacob, and Jacob became the father of twelve sons, who were the twelve fathers of Israel.

The fathers of Israel were jealous of Joseph, so they sold him to some people in Egypt. But God was with Joseph. He gave him safety during the times when he had great trouble, and He gave him favor and wisdom in the presence of Pharoah, the king of Egypt. Pharoah made Joseph the ruler over Egypt and over all of his house.

There was a time when none of Egypt or Canaan had any food, and the people there suffered very much. Our fathers did not have food, and Jacob sent them to Egypt when he heard there was grain there. It was their first visit to Egypt. During their second visit, Joseph told his brothers that he was their brother, so then Joseph's family became known to Pharoah. Then Joseph sent for his father Jacob, and all of his family members. There were seventy-five of them. Jacob went down into Egypt, and he and our fathers died there. They were carried over to Shechem, and they were buried in the place that Abraham bought from Hamor's sons in Shechem.

The time for the promise that God made to Abraham came near, and the number of people increased in Egypt. Another king, who did not know Joseph, began to rule over Egypt. He tricked our people and did evil things to our fathers, and forced them to throw their babies outside so they would not live. Moses was born at that time, and he was a beautiful and special child, and he was cared for in his father's house for three months. When he had to be put outside of his home, Pharoah's daughter took him and cared for him just like he was her own son. Moses was taught all the wisdom of the Egyptians and he was great in his words and his actions.

But when he was nearly forty years old he decided to visit his brothers, the people of Israel. Moses tried to help one of them when he saw an Egyptian doing things to him that harmed him, and Moses punished the Egyptian and killed him. Moses thought his brothers understood that God was going to use him to save them. But they did not understand. The next day he came to two Israelites who were fighting. He tried to bring peace between them and said, "Men, you are brothers. Why do you harm each other?" But the man who harmed his neighbor pushed Moses away and said, "Who made you a ruler and a judge over us? Do you want to kill me like you killed the Egyptian yesterday?" Moses ran away when he heard this, and he went to live as a stranger in the country of Midian, where his two sons were born.

At the end of forty years, an angel appeared to Moses in the wilderness, near the mountain named Sinai. The angel appeared in fire from a small burning bush. Moses was full of wonder because of what he saw, and the voice of the Lord spoke as Moses went near to look at the bush. The Lord said, 'I am the God of your fathers, the God of Abraham, Isaac, and Jacob.' Moses' body shook and he did not look, because he was full of fear. The Lord said to him, 'Take off your shoes because the place where you are standing is holy ground. I have seen the suffering of My people who are in Egypt. I have heard their cries and I have come down to Egypt to save them. Come now, I will send you back into Egypt.'

This Moses is the same man whom they rejected and to whom they said, 'Who made you a ruler and a judge?' But God sent him to be both their ruler and the person to save them. He did this with the help of the angel who appeared to Moses in the bush. Moses led them out from Egypt, after he had done wonders and miracles there and at the Red Sea and for forty years in the wilderness.

This is the Moses who said to the people of Israel, 'God will give you a prophet like me from among your brothers.' He was together with our fathers in the wilderness, and he was with the angel who spoke to him in the mountain named Sinai. He received living words to give to us.

But our fathers did not obey him, and they rejected him and turned their hearts to Egypt again. They said to Aaron, 'Make for us gods who will go ahead of us, because we do not know what has happened to Moses who led us out from Egypt.' So at that time they made an idol. It was a young cow. Then they brought a sacrifice to this idol, and they had great joy because of this thing that they had made with their hands. But God turned away from them and let them worship the stars in the sky. This is what was written in the book of the prophets.

It said, 'O Israel, did you offer me sacrifices and animals that were killed when you were in the wilderness for forty years? No, you took with you the tabernacle of Moloch, and the star of the god Rephan. You made these idols so you could worship them. Because of this, I will take you away, even farther than Babylon.'

Our fathers had the Tabernacle of Witness with them in the wilderness. It was made just like God had ordered Moses, when He spoke to him and told him that he should make it just like he had seen it. Later, our fathers received this tabernacle. They brought it with them when they went with Joshua and took the land of the nations whose people God had forced to leave before our fathers came. The tabernacle remained there until the time of David. God was very pleased with David, and David asked God to let him find a place for the God of Jacob to live. But it was Solomon who built Him the house. But the Most High God does not live in houses made by human hands. The prophet says: 'The heaven is my throne, and the earth is the place to rest my feet. What kind of house will you build for me?' says the Lord. 'Or where will the place be where I will rest? Didn't my hand make all these things?'

You are a hard group of people, who are not circumcised in your hearts and ears! You always do things that are against the Holy Spirit, just like your fathers did. Are there any of the prophets that your fathers did not persecute? They killed the prophets who told about the Righteous One who would come, and now you have betrayed Him and have killed Him. You were the ones who received the Law that the angels brought, but you did not obey it."

They were filled with great anger when they heard this, and they made angry sounds at Stephen with their teeth. But he was full of the Holy Spirit, and he looked up into heaven and saw the glory of God.

He also saw Jesus standing at the right side of God, and he said, "Look! I see heaven open, and the Son of man standing on the right side of God!" But they covered their ears with their hands and they called out with loud voices as they all rushed toward him. They threw him out of the city and began to stone him. The witnesses took off their coats and left them near a young man named Saul.

Stephen prayed to the Lord as they stoned him, "Lord Jesus, receive my spirit." He fell on his knees and called out in a loud voice, "Lord, do not hold this sin against them." He died after he said this.

Saul agreed that the death of Stephen was right.

A great persecution against the church in Jerusalem began on that day. All the people went to different places in all the areas of Judea and Samaria, except the apostles. Faithful men buried Stephen and were deeply sad because of him.

But Saul began to destroy the church. He went into every house, and took men and women and put them into prison.

Acts 7:1-8:3

We should never be afraid of what people might say or do, because when Christ is our Lord the Holy Spirit is always ready to give us the strength and wisdom we need. The Apostle Peter wrote:

"Who will harm you if you strongly desire to do the things that are good? But you are blessed when you suffer for doing what is

right. Do not fear what people say they will do to you, and do not be troubled. But, be sure you make Christ Lord in your hearts. Always be ready to answer everyone who asks you a reason for the hope that is in you. But do it with gentleness and respect. Be sure your reasons are right whenever you do anything, so the people who speak evil against your good way of life in Christ can be ashamed."

1 Peter 3:13-16

DISCUSSION SUGGESTIONS:

1. We have the same tool Stephen used to answer his accusers. What is it?

2. What should we remember when we need to tell others about Jesus? (Read Psalm 119:46-48 and Luke 21:14-15)

WRONG MOTIVES

So the persecuted people who went to different places went out and preached the message.

Philip went to the city of Samaria and preached about Christ to the people there. The crowd joined together and listened carefully to the things Philip spoke, when they heard and saw the miracles he did.

Many people had evil spirits and the spirits called out with loud voices as they came out from them. Many people who could not move their bodies and people who were crippled were healed. There was much joy in that city.

But there was a man named Simon who used to do magic in the city. He caused the people of Samaria to think he was someone great. Both the least important and the most important people all listened carefully to him and they said, "This man is the power of God that is known as the Great Power." They listened to him because he had filled them with wonder for a long time when he did magic.

But both men and women were baptized, when they believed Philip as he preached the good news about the kingdom of God and the name of Jesus Christ. Simon also believed and was baptized. He followed Philip and was full of wonder because of the signs and great miracles he saw.

The apostles who were at Jerusalem sent Peter and John to Samaria when they heard the people there had accepted the message of God.

When they came there, Peter and John prayed for the people so they could receive the Holy Spirit. The people had only been baptized in the name of the Lord Jesus, but the Holy Spirit had not come to any of them yet. They received the Holy Spirit after Peter and John laid their hands on them.

Simon offered them money when he saw that the Holy Spirit could be given to people when the apostles laid their hands on them. He said, "Give this power to me also, so people will receive the Holy Spirit when I lay my hands on them."

But Peter said to him, "Your money should die with you, because you thought you could buy the gift of God with money. You cannot be a part of our work or share it with us, because your heart is not right toward God. So repent of your evil plan and pray that the Lord will forgive you for this thought that is in your heart, because I see that you are full of hate, and you are under the control of sin." Simon answered, "Pray to the Lord for me, so the things you have said will not happen to me."

They returned to Jerusalem after they had told people their testimony and spoken about the message of the Lord, and they preached the gospel in many Samaritan towns.

Acts 8:4-25

It is natural for people to think they can earn or buy the things they want. But the gift of God is not like that. The Apostle Peter wrote:

"You know you were not saved with things that can be destroyed, like silver or gold, from your useless way of life that you inherited from your fathers. But you were saved by the

blood of Jesus Christ that has great value. He was like a lamb that was pure and perfect. God chose Him before the world was made, but He has appeared in these last times for your benefit. You are believers in God through Him. God brought Him back to life from death and gave Him glory, so your faith and hope are in God."

1 Peter 1:18-21

Discussion Suggestions:

1. What was Simon's motive in offering money to the disciples?

2. What did the disciples say about trying to buy the gift of God? What does this say to us? (Read 1 Corinthians 2:12)

PHILIP'S MISSION

But an angel of the Lord spoke to Philip, "Get up and go to the south, to the desert road that goes from Jerusalem to Gaza."

So he got up and went there.

A man from Ethiopia had come to Jerusalem to worship. Candace, the queen of Ethiopia, had given him much authority, and he was the manager of all of her riches. As he returned, he sat in his chariot and read the book of the prophet Isaiah.

The Spirit said to Philip, "Go and stay near to this chariot."

So Philip ran to the man, and heard him reading the book of Isaiah the prophet.

Philip said, "Do you understand what you are reading?"

He said, "How can I understand it, unless someone explains it to me?" He asked Philip to come and sit with him.

The part of the Word of God he read was this, "He was like a sheep that is led away to be killed, and like a lamb that does not make any sound before its wool is cut off from its body. So He did not open His mouth to speak. He was shamed, and the right kind of judgment was not given to Him. His life on earth ended. So who will be able to speak about His descendants?"

The Ethiopian said to Philip, "Please tell me who this prophet is speaking about? Is it about himself or about another person?"

Then Philip began to speak. He began at this part of the Word of God, and he preached to him about Jesus.

They came to some water as they went on their way and the

Ethiopian said, "Look, here is some water. Why shouldn't I be baptized?"

He ordered the chariot to be stopped, and both Philip and the man went down into the water, and Philip baptized him.

When they came out from the water, the Spirit of the Lord took Philip away.

The Ethiopian did not see him anymore, but he went on his way and had great joy.

But Philip appeared at Azotus and he went through the cities and preached the gospel until he came to Caesarea.

Acts 8:26-8:40

The man from Ethiopia did not understand that God had a plan for his life. So God sent Philip to tell him how he could be saved. The Apostle Paul wrote about the only way to receive salvation:

> *"You are saved by grace, through your faith. You did not do this by yourselves. It is a gift from God. It is not because of the things we do, so no one can be proud. We are what God has made us to be. In Christ Jesus, we are made for good works God has already planned for us to do."*

Ephesians 2:8-10

DISCUSSION SUGGESTIONS:

1. The angel of the Lord told Philip to leave a powerful ministry in Samaria and go to the desert. How did Philip react?

2. What did Philip do that helped the Ethiopian believe and be baptized? How do people come to have faith? (Read Romans 10:17)

SAUL BECOMES A NEW MAN

But Saul was still giving threats and desiring to kill the followers of the Lord.

He went to the high priest, and asked for letters from him to the synagogues in Damascus, so if he found any men and women there who belonged to the Way, he could put chains on them and bring them to Jerusalem.

As he came near to Damascus, suddenly a light from heaven shone all around him.

He fell on the ground and heard a voice say to him, "Saul, Saul, why do you persecute Me?"

He said, "Lord, who are You?"

He said, "I am Jesus whom you persecute. Get up and go into the city and you will be told what you must do."

The men who travelled with him stood there, but they were not able to say anything, because they heard the voice but they did not see anyone. Saul got up from the ground, but when he opened his eyes he could not see anything.

They took his hand and brought him to Damascus. He could not see for three days, and he did not eat or drink anything.

There was a follower of Jesus named Ananias at Damascus.

The Lord said to him in a vision, "Ananias."

He said, "Lord, I am here."

The Lord said to him, "Get up and go to the street named Straight. Go to Judas' house and ask for a man from Tarsus named

Saul. He is praying and he saw in a vision a man named Ananias come in and put his hands on him so he can see again."

But Ananias answered, "Lord, I have heard from many people about this man and about all the evil things he did to Your holy followers at Jerusalem. He has authority here from the chief priests to take to prison everyone who calls on Your name."

But the Lord said to him, "Go! I have chosen this man to do My work. He will take My name to the Gentiles, and kings, and the people of Israel. I will show him how much he must suffer because of My name."

Ananias left, and went into the house. He put his hands on Saul and said, "Brother Saul, the Lord Jesus, who appeared to you on the road when you came here, has sent me so you can see again and be filled with the Holy Spirit."

The things that had covered Saul's eyes fell off immediately, and he could see again.

He got up and was baptized, and he became strong after he ate some food.

Paul stayed for a few days with the followers at Damascus. He started to preach immediately in the synagogues. He preached that Jesus is the Son of God.

All the people who heard him were full of wonder and said, "Isn't he the man who was in Jerusalem and who tried to destroy the people who call on this name? Didn't he come here to put chains on them and bring them to the chief priests?"

But Saul increased in power, and the Jews who lived in Damascus were not able to argue with him any more, because he proved that Jesus is the Christ.

After many days the Jews met together and thought of a plan to kill him. But Saul heard about their plan. They watched the gates all day and all night, so they could kill him. But Saul's followers took him during the night and put him in a basket, and brought him down through an open place in the wall.

When he came to Jerusalem, Saul tried to join the followers of Jesus, but all of them were afraid of him. They did not believe he was a follower. But Barnabas took him and brought him to the apostles. He told them that Saul had seen the Lord on the road to Damascus and that the Lord had spoken to him, and that he had preached in the name of Jesus there and was not afraid.

Saul stayed with them and went freely in all parts of Jerusalem, and he preached in the name of the Lord and was not afraid. He spoke and argued with the Greek Jews, but they tried to kill him. The brothers brought him down to Caesarea when they heard about it, and they sent him to Tarsus.

So the church everywhere in Judea, Galilee, and Samaria had peace and became strong.

The number of people increased as they lived in the fear of the Lord and the comfort of the Holy Spirit.

Acts 9:1-31

God has a special purpose for each of us. Saul had a place in God's plan for the salvation of the world. Later, when he became the Apostle Paul, he wrote about this:

"The Gentiles will also receive God's inheritance along with His people, and they are members of the same group and receive the same promise of union with Jesus Christ, through the gospel. I was made a servant of the gospel by the gift of God's grace that was given to me by the working of His power. Even though I am less important than the least important of

*God's people, I was given this grace so I could preach to the
Gentiles the riches of Christ, that are too great to understand
completely, and to cause all people to see what God's mystery is.
God, who made all things, has hidden His mystery in the past.
He did this so His wisdom, that has many forms, can now be
made known to the rulers and the powers in the heavenly
places, through the church. This is the everlasting purpose that
He planned through Jesus Christ our Lord. We have courage in
union with Him, and we can come to God and be sure He
accepts us, because of our faith in Christ."*

Ephesians 3:6-12

DISCUSSION SUGGESTIONS:

1. What hard thing did God ask Ananias to do?

2. What did God tell Ananias about His purpose for Saul? Does
God have a similar purpose for us? (Read 1 Peter 2:9)

A GIFT OF LIFE

When Peter travelled to all parts of the country, he also went to visit the believers at Lydda.

He found a man there named Aeneas, who had been in bed for eight years because he could not move his body.

Peter said to Aeneas, "Jesus Christ heals you. Get up and make your bed."

He got up immediately. Everyone who lived at Lydda and Sharon saw him, and all of them turned to the Lord.

There was a follower of Christ in Joppa named Tabitha, (that means Dorcas). This woman did many good things for people and always helped the poor people.

She became sick at that time, and she died. After they had washed her, they put her in a room in the top part of the house.

Lydda was near Joppa, and the followers of Christ heard that Peter was there, so they sent two men to Joppa to say strongly to Peter, "Come immediately."

Peter got up and went with them.

When he came, they brought him into the room in the top part of the house, and all the widows stood near him and cried.

They showed Peter the coats and clothes that Tabitha made when she was with them. But Peter sent all of them out from the room, and he went down on his knees and prayed.

He turned toward the woman's body and said, "Tabitha, get up."

She opened her eyes, and she sat up when she saw Peter. Then Peter took her hand and helped her stand.

He called the believers and widows to come. He showed her to them, and she was alive.

It became known everywhere in Joppa, and many people believed in the Lord. Peter stayed in Joppa for many days with a tanner named Simon.

Acts 9:32-43

The apostles knew these great miracles were done only because of God's power working in them, so people could see that Jesus Christ truly is the Son of God. Paul wrote about this in his letter to the Ephesians:

> *"He is able to do much more than we can ever ask for or think of, by His power that works in us. Let glory be given to Him in the church and in Jesus Christ through all generations forever."*

Ephesians 3:20-21

DISCUSSION SUGGESTIONS:

1. What did Peter do after he sent everyone out of the room where Dorcas' body was lying?

2. What does this teach us about the source of this great miracle? (Read Ephesians 1:19-20)

THE GOD OF EVERYONE

There was a man in Caesarea named Cornelius. He was a captain of the group of soldiers named the Italian Regiment. He was a faithful man, and he and everyone in his house feared God. He gave much money to people who needed it, and he prayed to God often.

Cornelius clearly saw an angel from God come to him in a vision at about three o'clock in the afternoon.

The angel said, "Cornelius." He looked at him and he was afraid and he said, "Lord, what is it?"

The angel said to him, "God has remembered your prayers and the money you gave to the poor people. Now send men to Joppa and bring back a man named Simon, who is also named Peter. He is staying with a tanner named Simon. His house is near the sea."

When the angel who spoke to him had gone, Cornelius called two of his house servants and a soldier who was a religious man. He sent them to Joppa after he told them everything that happened.

They were travelling the next day, and as they came near the city, Peter went to the top of the house to pray, at about noon. He became hungry and wanted to eat. But a vision came to him while the people were making the food ready.

He saw heaven opened and something like a large sheet came down. It was lowered down to the earth by its four corners, and in it were all kinds of animals with four legs, reptiles, and birds from the sky.

A voice came to him and said, "Peter, get up. Kill and eat."

But Peter said, "No, Lord, I have never eaten anything that is unholy and unclean."

The voice spoke to him again. It said, "Do not think anything is unholy that God has made clean."

This happened three times and immediately the sheet was taken up into heaven.

While Peter was very troubled in his mind about the meaning of the vision he had seen, the men whom Cornelius sent had asked where Simon's house was, and they stood at the gate. They called out and asked if Simon, who was also named Peter, lived there.

The Spirit said to Peter, as he thought about the vision, "Three men are looking for you. So get up and go down. Go with them and don't have any doubts, because I have sent them."

Peter went down to where the men were and said, "I am the man you are looking for. Why did you come?"

They said, "Cornelius is a captain, and he is a righteous man who fears God. The whole nation of the Jews respects him. A holy angel told him to send men to bring you to his house and to listen to what you say."

Then Peter asked them to come in to be his guests. He got up the next day and went with them. Some of the brothers from Joppa also went with him.

Peter and the others came into Caesarea the next day. Cornelius was waiting for them, and he had called together his family members and some friends whom he knew very well. Cornelius met Peter as he came into the house, and Cornelius fell down at his feet and worshiped him.

But Peter helped him get up and said, "Stand up, because I am also only a man."

Peter talked with him, and he went inside and found many

people who had come together there.

Peter said to them, "You know it is against the law for a Jewish man to be with a Gentile or to visit a Gentile. But God has shown me that I should not say that any person is unholy or unclean. That is why I came, and I did not argue when I was asked to come. So I ask you, why did you send for me?"

Cornelius said, "Four days ago at this time, I prayed in my house. It was three o'clock in the afternoon. A man who wore bright clothes stood in front of me. He said, 'Cornelius, your prayer has been heard and God has remembered the money you gave to the poor people. So send men to Joppa and ask for Simon, who is also named Peter. He is staying in the house of a tanner named Simon, who lives near the sea.' So I sent for you immediately, and you have been kind and have come. Now we are all here in the presence of God to hear everything the Lord has ordered you to tell us."

So Peter began to speak, "I am sure now that God does not show special favor to any person, but He accepts every person from every nation who fears Him and who does what is right. You know the message God sent to the children of Israel that tells good news about peace through Jesus Christ, who is the Lord of all. You know what happened everywhere in Judea, that started in Galilee after the baptism that John preached. God anointed Jesus of Nazareth with the Holy Spirit and with power. He went around and did good things, and He healed all the people who were troubled by Satan, because God was with Jesus. We are witnesses of all the things He did in the country of the Jews and in Jerusalem. They killed Him when they hanged Him on a tree, but God brought Him back to life from death on the third day. Not all the people saw Him, only the people whom God had chosen to see Him. We saw Him. We ate and drank with Him after He was brought back to life from death. He ordered us to preach to the people and to tell them that

He is the One whom God chose to be the Judge of all the people who are alive and all the people who are dead. All the prophets spoke about Him, and said that everyone who believes in Him will receive forgiveness from sins through His name."

While Peter spoke these words, the Holy Spirit fell on all of them who heard the message.

The circumcised believers who came with Peter were greatly surprised because the gift of the Holy Spirit was also poured out on the Gentiles. They heard them praise God and speak in other languages.

Peter answered, "Can anyone say these people should not be baptized in water? They have received the Holy Spirit just as we have."

So Peter ordered that they be baptized in the name of Jesus Christ. Then they asked Peter to stay with them for a few days.

Acts 10:1-48

God had to teach the early believers that all of us are the same in His sight. One way He did this was by giving the Holy Spirit to people that the Jewish Christians had thought were not good enough. Paul wrote about this to the Corinthians and the Ephesians:

> "We were all baptized into one body by one Spirit, whether we are Jews or Greeks, slaves or free people, and we were all given one Spirit."

1 Corinthians 12:13

"Do everything you can to keep the unity that the Spirit gives by the peace that causes you to be kept together. There is one body and one Spirit, just as there is one hope that God has called you to. There is one Lord, one faith, and one baptism. There is one God and Father of everything. He rules everything, He is everywhere, and He is in everything."

Ephesians 4:3-6

DISCUSSION SUGGESTIONS:

1. What happened after Peter told the household of Cornelius about Jesus?

2. How did the Jewish believers know that the Gentiles had received the Holy Spirit and what did that prove to them? (Read Galatians 3:26-29)

HELPING BROTHERS

The apostles and the brothers who were in Judea heard that the Gentiles had also received the message of God. So the circumcised believers argued with Peter when he came up to Jerusalem.

They said, "You went to the house of men who are not circumcised and ate with them."

So Peter explained everything to them in the order that it happened, and said, "I was praying in the city of Joppa, and I saw a vision. Something like a large sheet came down. It was lowered down from heaven by its four corners. It came down to me, and I looked closely into it and saw animals with four legs from the earth, wild animals, reptiles, and birds from the sky. I also heard a voice say to me, Peter, get up. Kill and eat.' But I said, 'No, Lord, because I have never put anything unholy or unclean in my mouth.' But the voice from heaven said a second time, 'Do not think anything is unholy that God has made clean.' This happened three times and everything was taken up again into heaven. Immediately three men who had been sent to me from Caesarea stood in front of the house where I was staying. The Spirit told me to go with them and not to have any doubts. These six brothers also came with me, and we went into the man's house. He told us that he saw an angel standing in his house, and the angel said, 'Send men to Joppa to bring Simon, who is also named Peter. He will speak a message to you that will save you and the people in your house.' The Holy Spirit came upon them as I began to speak, just like He came to us the first time. I remembered what the Lord had said, 'It is true that John baptized with water, but you will be baptized with the Holy Spirit.' Who was I to go against God if He gave to them the same gift He gave to us after we believed in the Lord Jesus Christ?"

They were quiet when they heard these things, and they praised God. They said, "God has also given the Gentiles the opportunity to repent and have life."

Those who had left and gone to different places because of the persecution that came at the time of Stephen, travelled as far as Phoenicia, Cyprus, and Antioch. They did not speak the message to any people except the Jews.

But there were some men from Cyprus and Cyrene who came to Antioch. They also spoke to the Greeks and preached the Lord Jesus. The Lord was with them and a great number of people believed and turned to the Lord.

The church in Jerusalem heard about them, and they sent Barnabas to Antioch. When he came, he saw the grace of God, and had great joy. He encouraged all of them, and told them to decide in their hearts to remain faithful to the Lord. Barnabas was a good man and was full of the Holy Spirit and faith, and many people believed in the Lord.

Barnabas went to Tarsus to look for Saul, and he brought him to Antioch when he found him. They met together with the church there for a whole year and they taught many people. The followers of Christ in Antioch were the first people to be named Christians.

Some prophets came down from Jerusalem to Antioch during this time. One of them, named Agabus, stood and the Spirit told him to say that there would be a great need for food in all the world. This happened during the time when Claudius was the ruler.

Every follower of Christ decided to send as much as he could to help the brothers who lived in Judea. They did this by giving their gifts to Barnabas and Saul to take to the church leaders.

Acts 11:1-30

God taught the early Jewish Christians how wrong it was to think they deserved to be Christians more than others did. They learned to love each other just because they were brothers and sisters in Christ. Both Paul and Peter wrote about this later:

"I speak to every person who is among you, by the grace that is given to me. Do not think more highly of yourself than you should, but think about yourself with true judgment just as God has given a certain amount of faith to each person. In the same way, we are many people who are one body in Christ and each person belongs to all the others."

Romans 12:3,5

"You are believers in God through Him [Jesus Christ] ... You have obeyed the truth and made your souls pure so you would be able to truly love your brothers. So love each other deeply from your hearts."

1 Peter 1:21-22

DISCUSSION SUGGESTIONS:

1. What did the critical Jewish believers do to show their change of heart toward the Gentile believers in Antioch?

2. What did the Gentile Christians in Antioch do that showed their attitude toward the Jewish Christians in Judea? What does this teach about being Christians? (Read John 13:35 and 1 John 3:16-18)

WEEK 3

A KING IS JUDGED

At about this time, King Herod took some of the people who belonged to the church, so he could persecute them.

He killed James, the brother of John, with a sword, and when he saw that this had pleased the Jews, he also took Peter. This was during the time of the Feast of Unleavened Bread.

He put Peter in prison after he had taken him, and four groups of soldiers guarded him. Herod's plan was to bring Peter out to the people after the Passover.

So they kept Peter in the prison, but the church prayed strongly to God about him.

The night before Herod was going to bring him out, Peter was sleeping between two soldiers, and there were two chains on his body. There were also guards at the door of the prison.

Suddenly, an angel from the Lord appeared, and a light shone in the prison room. He hit the side of Peter's body to wake him and said, "Get up quickly," and Peter's chains fell off his hands. The angel said to him, "Put on your clothes and your shoes."

Peter did this, and the angel said to him, "Put on your coat and follow me." Peter went out and followed him, and he did not know that the things the angel was doing were real. Peter thought he was seeing a vision. After they went past the first and second guard gates, they came to the iron gate that led into the city. The gate opened by itself and they went out. They went along a street, and immediately the angel went away from him.

When Peter understood what had just happened, he said, "I know now that it is true that the Lord has sent His angel and saved me from Herod and from all that the Jewish people expected to happen."

Peter came to Mary's house after he understood what had happened. Mary was the mother of John, who was also named Mark.

Many people were there together, and they were praying. A servant girl named Rhoda came when Peter knocked at the door of the gate. When she knew it was Peter's voice, she had great joy. She did not open the gate, but instead she ran in and told them that Peter was at the gate. They said to her, "Your mind is not right." But she said strongly that it was true. They said, "Then it is his angel." But Peter continued to knock. They were full of wonder when they opened the gate and saw him.

But he made a sign to them with his hand that told them to be quiet, and he told them that the Lord had brought him out of the prison. Peter said, "Tell these things to James and the brothers." Then he went away to another place.

The soldiers were greatly troubled the next morning about what had happened to Peter. Herod looked for him and did not find him, and he asked the guards about him. He ordered his men to kill the guards.

Then Herod went down from Judea to Caesarea and stayed there for a while. Herod was very angry at the people of Tyre and Sidon. They came to him together, and asked for peace, after they had become friends with the king's personal servant, Blastus. They did this because their country received food from the king's country.

Herod put on his special king's clothes on the day that had been chosen and he sat on his throne, and spoke a message to the people. The people shouted and said, "This is the voice of a god and not a man." Immediately an angel from the Lord caused Herod to become sick, because he did not give honor to God. Worms ate him and he died.

But God's message continued to grow and spread to more places. Barnabas and Saul returned from Jerusalem when they had finished the things they went there to do, and they took John, who was also named Mark, with them.

Acts 12:1-25

God's promise to be with everyone who shares His Word with others is as true today as it was for the early Christians. The Apostle Paul wrote:

"The Lord stood with me and gave me strength, so the message could be fully preached through me, and all the Gentiles can hear it. I was saved from the lion's mouth. The Lord will save me from every evil act, and will bring me safely to His heavenly kingdom. Glory should be given to Him forever. Amen."

2 Timothy 4:17-18

DISCUSSION SUGGESTIONS:

1. What did the church do when Peter was put in jail and how did they react when the servant said Peter was at the door? Why are we sometimes surprised when our prayers are answered?

2. Peter was one man in a locked prison, guarded by many soldiers. What should his escape help us remember? (Read Hebrews 13:6 and 2 Corinthians 1:8-10)

THE MESSAGE OF LIFE

There were some prophets and teachers at the church in Antioch. They were Barnabas, Simeon who was also named Niger, Lucius of Cyrene, Manaen, who was from the family of Herod the king, and Saul.

While they worshiped the Lord and fasted, the Holy Spirit said to them, "Set apart Barnabas and Saul to do the work I have asked them to do."

Then they laid their hands on them, and sent them away, after they fasted and prayed.

So both of them who were sent out by the Holy Spirit went down to Seleucia. They sailed to Cyprus from there. They preached the message of God in the Jewish synagogue when they were at Salamis, and John was also with them to help them.

They travelled through all of the island and came to Paphos. They found a Jewish man there who was a false prophet and who did magic. His name was Bar-Jesus, and he worked for the ruler, Sergius Paulus, who was an intelligent man.

This ruler sent for Barnabas and Saul because he wanted to hear God's message. But Elymas, the man who did magic (this is what his name also means) went against them, and tried to turn the ruler away from the faith.

But Saul, who was also named Paul, was filled with the Holy Spirit and he looked directly at him and said, "You are full of lies and tricks, and you are the son of Satan. You are an enemy of everything that is right. Will you never stop changing the true and right ways of the Lord? The hand of the Lord is on you, and you will be blind and will not be able to see the sun for a time."

Immediately a dark mist covered Elymas' eyes and he went around to try to find someone to take his hand and lead him. The ruler was full of wonder because of the teaching about the Lord and he became a believer when he saw what had happened.

Paul and the people who were with him sailed from Paphos and came to Perga in Pamphylia. John went away from them and returned to Jerusalem. But they continued and went on from Perga and came to Antioch in Pisidia.

Paul and the people who were with him went into the synagogue on the Sabbath day and sat there. The rulers of the synagogue sent them a message after some things from the law and the books of the prophets were read.

They said, "Brothers, please speak if you have a message that would help the people."

Paul stood and made a sign to them with his hand and said, "Men of Israel and people who fear God, listen to me. The God of the people of Israel chose our fathers, and made the people great when they lived in the land of Egypt, and He led them out from Egypt with great power. He was patient with them for about forty years in the wilderness. He destroyed seven nations in Canaan, and gave their land to His people for four hundred and fifty years. After this, He gave them judges until the time of Samuel, the prophet.

Then they asked for a king and God gave them Saul, who ruled for forty years. He was Kish's son, a man from Benjamin's tribe. God made David their king after He took Saul away. He also said this about David, 'I have seen that David, the son of Jesse, is a man close to my heart. He is a man who will do everything I want him to do.' God brought to Israel a Savior, Jesus, from the family line of this man, just as He promised.

Before Jesus came, John preached to all the people of Israel that baptism means repenting. At the time that John was finishing his work, he said, 'Who do you think I am? I am not He. But He will come later. I am not even good enough to take off His shoes.'

Brothers, children from the family line of Abraham, and those who fear God, the message of salvation has been sent to us. The people in Jerusalem and their rulers did not know Him. But they caused the things that the prophets had said, that are read on every Sabbath day, to become true when they condemned Him.

They asked Pilate to put Him to death, although they could not find a reason to put Him to death. They took Him down from the cross and put Him in a grave, after they had done all the things that were written about Him. But God brought Him back to life from death, and the people who came from Galilee to Jerusalem with Him saw Him for many days. They are the people who tell other people about Him now.

We bring you good news about this promise that was made to the fathers and that has become true for your children.

God brought Jesus back to life, as it is written in the second Psalm, 'You are my Son, and I have become your Father today.' God brought Him back to life from death and He will never return to be destroyed by death. God said this in these words, 'I will give you the holy and sure blessings that were promised to David.'

God also said in another psalm, 'You will not let your Holy One be destroyed in the grave.' David died and was buried with his fathers after he finished God's purpose for him in his generation, and he was destroyed in the grave. But the One God brought back to life was not destroyed in the grave.

So brothers, you must know for sure that the message about forgiveness of sins is made known to you because of Him, and everyone who believes is made free by Him, from all the things from which you could not be made free by the law of Moses. So be careful, so that the things the prophets said will not happen to you: 'Look, you people who doubt, and be filled with wonder and die, because I will do something during your time, something that you will not believe even if someone told you.'"

As Paul and Barnabas went out, the people asked them to speak more about these things on the next Sabbath day.

After the meeting, Paul and Barnabas were followed by many Jews and by many Gentiles who had become faithful believers. Paul and Barnabas spoke to them, and urged them to continue living in the grace of God. Almost all of the people in the city came to hear God's message on the next Sabbath day.

The Jews were filled with jealousy when they saw the crowd of people, and they began to argue against the things Paul talked about, and to say evil things.

Paul and Barnabas spoke without fear and said, "It was necessary for the message of God to be spoken to you people first. But we turn to the Gentiles now because you do not accept the message of God, and because of this, you judge yourselves not to deserve everlasting life. We do this because the Lord has commanded us and said, 'I have made you a light to the Gentiles, so you would show salvation to the farthest places on the earth.'"

The Gentiles had great joy when they heard this, and they gave honor to God's message. All the people who were chosen to have everlasting life became believers. The Lord's message spread everywhere in all the area.

But the Jews caused the important religious women and the leaders of the city to be troubled about this, and caused persecution to begin against Paul and Barnabas. They forced them to leave their area.

But Paul and Barnabas shook off the dust from their feet as a sign against them and went to Iconium.

The followers of Christ were filled with joy and with the Holy Spirit.

Acts 13:1-52

When the Jews did not accept God's message about Jesus Christ, it caused great pain to the apostle Paul. He wrote about this in his letter to the Romans:

"I am telling the truth in Christ. I do not lie. My conscience, that is ruled by the Holy Spirit, also tells me I am not lying when I say that I have great sadness and pain in my heart that does not stop. I could wish that I were condemned and separated from Christ because of my brothers who are from the same bloodline and are Israelites. He made them his children and showed His glory to them, He made His agreements with them and gave them the law. They have the true worship of God and they have received God's promises. The fathers belong to them and Christ comes from this family. He is God over all things and is praised forever. Amen."

Romans 9:1-5

DISCUSSION SUGGESTIONS:

1. What message did Paul say had been sent to the family line of Abraham?

2. What did Paul say must happen when the Jews did not receive the message of God? Who can receive the message about forgiveness of sins? (Read John 3:16 and Colossians 3:11)

THE POWER IS FROM GOD

Paul and Barnabas went together into the synagogue of the Jews in Iconium, and a very large crowd of both Jews and Greeks became believers because of the way Paul and Barnabas spoke.

But the Jews who did not believe caused the Gentiles to be troubled, and to have bad thoughts in their minds against the brothers.

Paul and Barnabas stayed there a long time and spoke without fear about the Lord, who proved that the message about His grace was true, because He gave them the power to do miracles and wonders.

But the people from the city were divided, because some of them agreed with the Jews and others believed the apostles. The Gentiles and the Jews made a plan with their leaders to do bad things to Paul and Barnabas and to stone them. But Paul and Barnabas heard about it and went quickly to the cities of Lystra and Derbe in Lycaonia, and to places near there, and they preached the gospel there.

There was a man at Lystra whose feet were crippled. He had been crippled since the time he was born and had never walked. He listened to Paul as he spoke, and Paul looked closely at him and saw that he had faith to be healed.

Paul said with a loud voice, "Stand on your feet."

The crippled man jumped up and walked.

When the crowd of people saw what Paul had done, they

shouted in the Lycaonian language, "The gods have come down to us. They are like men!"

Then they named Barnabas "Zeus", and Paul "Mercury", because he was the chief speaker.

The priest of Zeus, who had a temple just outside the city, brought cows and flowers to the gates. He and the people in the crowd wanted to offer them as sacrifices to Barnabas and Paul.

The apostles tore their clothes when they heard about it, and they ran quickly into the middle of the crowd.

They called out, "Men, why do you do these things? We are only men, and human just like you. We bring you good news, that you should turn away from these useless things, and turn to a living God who made the heaven and the earth and the sea, and all that is in them. In the past, He let all the nations do whatever they wanted to do, but He still gave you things to show you who He is. He showed kindness when He gave you rain from heaven, and grain in the fields at the right times, and He gave you much food and filled your hearts with joy."

Even after they said these things, it was hard for Paul and Barnabas to stop the crowd of people from offering sacrifices to them.

Then some Jews came from Antioch and Iconium, and they convinced the crowd of people to stone Paul.

They pulled his body out of the city, because they thought he was dead.

But he got up while the followers were standing around him, and went into the city again.

He went to Derbe with Barnabas the next day, and they preached the gospel to the people in the city. Many people became followers of Christ.

Then they returned to Lystra, Iconium and Antioch, and they

gave strength to the hearts of the followers there.

They also encouraged them to continue in the faith and said, "We must endure many hard things if we want to go into the kingdom of God."

Paul and Barnabas chose leaders for the people in every church, and they prayed and fasted and put them in the care of the Lord in whom they believed.

Then Paul and Barnabas went through Pisidia and came to Pamphylia. After they had preached the message in Perga, they went down to Attalia.

They sailed from there to Antioch. This was the place where they had been put into the care of God's grace for the work they had now completed.

When Paul and Barnabas came, they told the people in the church to come together, and they told them all the things God had done through them, and that He had made a way for the Gentiles to become believers.

Then they stayed there with the followers for a long time.

Acts 14:1-28

A natural human tendency is to honor men who do great things. Paul knew that he could only do the great things he did because the power was from God. He wrote about it in his second letter to the Corinthian church:

"We do not preach about ourselves, but we preach about Christ Jesus as Lord, and we preach that we are your servants for Jesus. The God who said, 'Light will shine out of darkness,' is the same God who has put the light in our hearts of the knowledge

of God's glory, shining in the face of Christ. But we who have this great spiritual treasure are still like pots made of clay. This is to show that this great power is from God, and not from ourselves."

2 Corinthians 4:5-7

DISCUSSION SUGGESTIONS:

1. What did the people say when they saw the healing of the crippled man at Lystra?

2. What did Paul and Barnabas say about themselves? What should we always remember from this? (Read 2 Corinthians 3:5 and John 15:5)

ENCOURAGING, NOT JUDGING

Some men came from Judea. They taught the brothers and said, "You cannot be saved if you are not circumcised, because this is the tradition that Moses taught." Paul and Barnabas did not agree with this teaching, and they argued with them.

So Paul, Barnabas, and some other believers were chosen to go up to Jerusalem to ask the apostles and leaders about this question.

The people in the church sent them on their way, and they went through Phoenicia and Samaria, and told the brothers there about the Gentiles who had become believers. This caused all of them to be filled with great joy.

The people in the church, the apostles, and the leaders welcomed Paul, Barnabas and the others when they came to Jerusalem, and they told them all the things God had done through them.

But some believers who belonged to the group of the Pharisees stood and said, "The Gentiles must be circumcised, and they must be told to obey the laws of Moses."

The apostles and the leaders came together to think and talk about this.

After they had talked about it for a long time, Peter stood and said to them, "Brothers, you know that God chose me from among you a long time ago to speak the message of the gospel to the Gentiles, so they could hear it and become believers. God, who knows what is in people's hearts, showed them that He accepted them by giving the Holy Spirit to them just as He gave Him to us. He did not make any difference between us and them. He made their hearts clean because they believed. So why do you test God by putting a heavy weight on the backs of the followers, that even our fathers or we were not able to carry? But we believe we are saved through the grace of the Lord Jesus in the same way as they are saved."

Then all of them became quiet and listened as Barnabas and Paul told about the miracles and wonders God did through them among the Gentiles.

After they had spoken, James said, "Brothers, listen to me. Simon has told you that God first showed His care for the Gentiles by taking from among them some people for His name. This agrees with what the prophets wrote, 'I will return after these things, and I will build again the house of David that had fallen, and I will build again the parts of his house that were destroyed. I will make it strong again so all the rest of the people, and all the Gentiles who are called by My name, can seek the Lord. The Lord, who does these things that have been known from the beginning of time, says this.' So my judgment is that we should not trouble the people among the Gentiles who turn to God. But we should write to them and tell them not to eat food that is unclean because it has been offered to idols, to keep themselves away from sexual sin, and not to eat meat from animals that are strangled, and not to eat blood. We do this because Moses' laws have been preached about in every city since the earliest times, because they are read in the synagogues on every Sabbath day."

Then the apostles, leaders, and all the people of the church decided to choose some of their men and send them to Antioch with Paul and Barnabas. They chose Judas, who was also named Barsabas, and Silas. They were leaders among the brothers.

They wrote a letter and sent it with them.

It said, "Your brothers, the apostles and leaders, send greetings to the Gentile brothers who are in Antioch, Syria and Cilicia. We have heard that some of the people who came from our group have troubled your minds because of the things they said. We did not give them authority to do that. So all of us agreed to choose some men and send them to you with our dear friends, Barnabas and Paul. These are men who have let their lives be in danger for the name of our Lord Jesus Christ. So we have sent Judas and Silas, who will tell you exactly the same things we have written to you. It seemed good to the Holy Spirit and to us not to put any weights on you except these necessary things. You must not eat food that is offered to idols, blood, and meat from animals that are strangled, and you must keep yourselves away from sexual sin. You will do well if you keep yourselves away from these things. Farewell."

So the men were sent away and they went down to Antioch, and they asked everyone in the church to come together. Then they gave them the letter. They were full of joy when they read it, because the message encouraged them.

Judas and Silas, who were also prophets, said many things that encouraged the brothers and made them stronger. They stayed there awhile, and then the brothers sent them back in peace to the people who had sent them there. But Paul and Barnabas stayed there, and they taught and preached the message of the Lord, along with many other men.

Acts 15:1-35

The apostle Paul always taught very clearly that our salvation and the good works we do are because of God's grace and power in our lives. He wrote about this in his letter to the Ephesians:

"You are saved by grace, through your faith. You did not do this by yourselves. It is a gift from God. It is not because of the things we do. This is so no one can be proud. We are what God made us to be. We are made for good things God had already planned for us to do in Christ Jesus."

Ephesians 2:8-10

DISCUSSION SUGGESTIONS:

1. Why was it wrong for the Jewish believers to tell the Gentile Christians they must keep the law of Moses?

2. What would that be saying about Jesus' death and sacrifice? What is important to remember about how we are saved? (Read Titus 3:5 and 2 Timothy 1:9)

WHEN GOD GUIDES HE PROVIDES

After a long time, Paul said to Barnabas, "Let's return now to every city where we preached the Lord's message, and visit the brothers there and see how they are."

Barnabas wanted to take with them John, who was also named Mark.

But Paul thought it was not good to take Mark with them, because Mark went away from them when they were in Pamphylia, and did not continue with the work.

They did not agree about this, and so they separated from each other. So Barnabas took Mark with him and sailed to Cyprus. But Paul chose Silas and went away, after the brothers had given them to the care of the Lord's grace.

Paul went through Syria and Cilicia and made the churches stronger. Paul also came to Derbe and Lystra.

One of Christ's followers named Timothy was there. He was the son of a Jewish woman who was a believer, but his father was a Greek. The brothers at Lystra and Iconium said good things about him. Paul wanted Timothy to go with him, so he took him and circumcised him, because of the Jews who were there. Paul did this because all of them knew his father was a Greek.

As they went through the cities, they gave the people the decision that the apostles and leaders in Jerusalem made, so they could obey it. So the churches were made strong in the faith and their number increased every day.

They went through the area of Phrygia and Galatia, because the Holy Spirit did not allow them to preach the gospel in Asia.

They tried to go into Bithynia when they came to the edge of Mysia, but the Spirit of Jesus did not allow them to go there. So they went on past Mysia and came down to Troas.

Paul saw a vision in the night. There was a Macedonian man who stood there and asked him, "Come to Macedonia and help us." When Paul saw the vision, we made ourselves ready immediately and we went to Macedonia. We decided that God had called us to preach the gospel to them.

So we started to sail from Troas and went directly to Samothrace and to Neapolis, the next day. We sailed to Philippi, a city in Macedonia that was the first area under Roman rule. We waited in this city for several days.

On the Sabbath day we went outside the gate to a river where we thought there was a place to pray. We sat down and spoke to the women who came together. There was a woman named Lydia from the city of Thyatira who sold purple cloth. She was a woman who worshiped God. The Lord opened her heart as she listened, and she believed the things Paul spoke about.

After she and the people from her house were baptized, she asked us strongly, "Come and stay at my house, if you have decided that I am a faithful believer in the Lord," and she convinced us to go.

Acts 15:36-16:15

The apostle Paul always understood that he could not build the church himself. The Lord opened Lydia's heart just as the Lord opened the doors for Paul to preach the gospel. He spoke about this in his letter to the Colossians:

"Continue to pray faithfully. Keep your mind and thoughts clear as you pray, and thank God. Pray for us also and ask God to give us a good opportunity to preach His message about the mystery of Christ. It is because of this that I am in prison. Pray that I will make it known as clearly as I should."

Colossians 4:2-4

DISCUSSION SUGGESTIONS:

1. Did God have a plan about where Paul should go to preach the gospel and how did He make that plan known?

2. Who opened Lydia's heart to listen when Paul preached in Macedonia? Does God have a plan for each of our lives, and does He go ahead to prepare the way for us too? (Isaiah 48:17)

Pleasing God Rather than Man

A servant girl, who had a strange spirit in her, met us one day as we went to the place of prayer. She earned much money for her masters, because she was a fortune-teller.

She followed Paul and us, and she called out, "These men are servants of the Most High God. They are telling you about the way to be saved." She did this for many days.

But Paul was greatly troubled, and he turned and said to the spirit, "I order you in the name of Jesus to come out from her!"

It came out immediately.

The girl's masters took Paul and Silas and pulled them into the market place and took them to the rulers. They did this because they knew that their hope for getting money was gone.

When they had brought them to the Roman rulers, they said, "These men are Jews and they are causing much trouble in our city. They teach traditions that the law does not allow us, who are Romans, to accept or obey."

The crowd also joined together against Paul and Silas, and the Roman rulers tore off their clothes and ordered their men to beat them.

After they had beaten them badly, they threw them into prison and ordered the guard to watch them carefully. The guard threw them into the inner prison after he had received the order, and he put their feet tightly in stocks.

Paul and Silas were praying and singing songs of praise to God at about twelve o'clock that night, and the prisoners were listening to them. Suddenly there was a great earthquake, and the foundation of the prison shook. Immediately all the doors were opened, and everyone's chains became loose.

The guard woke from his sleep, and when he saw that the prison doors were opened, he took his sword and wanted to kill himself, because he thought the prisoners had run away.

But Paul called out with a loud voice, "Do not harm yourself, because we are all here!"

The guard asked for the lights to be turned on, and he ran in. He was shaking because of fear and he fell down in front of Paul and Silas.

Then he brought them out and said, "Men, what must I do to be saved?"

They said, "Believe in the Lord Jesus, and you and all the people in your family will be saved."

They spoke the Lord's message to him and all the people in his family. At that hour of the night, the guard took them and washed their wounds. He and his family were also baptized immediately. Then he brought them to his house and gave them food. The guard and all the people in his family had great joy, because they now believed in God.

The Roman rulers sent their officers the next morning, and said, "Let those men go."

The guard told Paul, "The Roman rulers have ordered me to let you go. So come out now, and go in peace."

But Paul said to the officers, "We are Romans, who were not proven to be guilty, but they publicly beat us, and threw us into prison. Now they want to take us out from prison secretly? No! They must come and bring us out!"

The officers told the Roman rulers what Paul said, and they

were afraid when they heard that Paul and Silas were Romans. So they went to Paul and Silas and talked to them in a very kind way. Then they brought them out and begged them to go away from the city.

Paul and Silas went to Lydia's house after they came out from prison, and they met the brothers and encouraged them. Then they went away from there.

Acts 16:16-40

Paul's life was a living example that those who follow Christ will be persecuted, but the Lord continued to deliver Paul. He reminded his young friend Timothy of this in his second letter:

"But you have followed my teaching, kind of life, purpose, faith, patience, love, endurance, and sufferings that happened to me at Antioch, Iconium and Lystra, and the persecutions I endured. The Lord saved me from all of them. It is true that everyone who wants to live a godly life in Jesus Christ will be persecuted."

2 Timothy 3:10-12

DISCUSSION SUGGESTIONS:

1. What did Paul and Silas do after they had been beaten and thrown in prison?

2. What good thing happened when they were put in jail? What should we remember if we face difficulties as Christians? (Read Isaiah 41:10 and Matthew 28:20)

STEADFAST IN SERVICE

After they went through Amphipolis and Apollonia, they came to Thessalonica, where there was a Jewish synagogue.

Paul went to them, just like he always did, and talked with them about the Word of God on three Sabbath days. He explained and proved to them that the Christ had to suffer and come back to life again from death.

He said, "This Jesus whom I preach to you is the Christ."

Some of them were convinced about this, and they joined Paul and Silas. A large number of Greeks who worshiped God, and many women leaders also, became believers and joined them.

But the Jews were jealous and they brought some evil men from the market place, and they all went together to cause great trouble in the city. They ran to Jason's house to bring out Paul and Silas, and give them to the crowd of angry people. But they did not find them, so they forced Jason and some other brothers to come, and they put them in front of the rulers.

They called out, "These men have caused great trouble in the rest of the world, and now they have come here. Jason welcomed these men who do things against Caesar's laws, and they say there is another king, named Jesus."

The crowd of people and the city's rulers were troubled when they heard these things. They took money from Jason and the other men, and then they let them go. The brothers immediately sent Paul and Silas away to Berea during the night.

When they came there, they went into the Jewish synagogue. The people were more respectable than those in Thessalonica, because they desired very much to receive the message, and they studied the Word of God every day, so they could know if what was said was true. Many of them became believers. Some important Greek women and many men also became believers.

But when the Jews in Thessalonica heard that Paul preached the message of God at Berea, they came there also, and they caused the people in the crowds to be troubled.

The brothers sent Paul out to the sea shore immediately, but Silas and Timothy stayed there.

The people who went with Paul brought him to Athens, and they were told to go and tell Silas and Timothy to come to Paul as soon as possible. So they went away from Athens.

Paul's spirit was troubled as he waited for them at Athens, because he saw that the city was full of idols. So he talked to the Jews in the synagogue. He also talked with the Greeks who worshiped God, and every day he talked to the people who were in the market place.

Some of the Epicurean and Stoic philosophers talked with him. Some of them said, "What is this person trying to say?" Others said, "It seems that he preaches about strange gods, because he preached about Jesus and that He was brought back to life from death."

They took Paul and brought him to the Areopagus and said to him, "Can we know what this new teaching is that you speak about? You bring some strange things for us to listen to, and we want to know what these things mean."

The Athenians and the strangers who lived there used all their time to tell about or listen to the newest ideas.

Paul stood in the middle of the Areopagus and said, "Men of Athens, I see you are very religious about all things. I went and looked at the things you worship, and I found an altar with these words written on it, 'To an unknown god.' So I will preach to you about the unknown god that you worship. The God who made the world and all the things in it is the Lord of heaven and earth. He does not live in temples made by hands. He is not served by people's hands. He doesn't need anything, because He is the One who gives life, breath and everything to people. He took one man and made from him all the kinds of people that live in all the earth, and He planned the times they would live and the places they would live. God did this so they would seek Him, and then they might reach out to Him and find Him, though He is not far from each of us. We live, move, and exist because of Him. Even some of your writers have said, 'We also are His children.' Since we are God's children, we should not think that God is like gold, silver or stone, that is made by man's art and thought. God overlooked the times of ignorance when men did not have the right knowledge, but He now commands all people everywhere to repent. He has chosen a day when He will judge the world with righteousness. He will do this through a Man whom He chose. He gave proof of this to all people when He brought Him back to life from death."

Some of the people laughed when they heard about being brought back to life from death. But other people said, "We want to hear about this from you again." So Paul went away from them.

But some men followed him and became believers. Dionysius the Areopagite was one of them. There was also a woman named Damaris, and some other people who were with them.

Acts 17:1-34

The apostle Paul had one message ... that Jesus Christ was crucified and came back to life again to save us from our sins. He made this clear in his first letter to the Corinthians:

"Brothers, I did not come with great words or wisdom when I came to you. But I preached the testimony about God to you because I decided not to know anything while I was with you, except Jesus Christ and His death on the cross. I was weak and shook because of fear when I was with you. My message and preaching were not with wise and convincing words, but to show the Spirit's power, so your faith would not depend on people's wisdom but on God's power."

1 Corinthians 2:1-5

DISCUSSION SUGGESTIONS:

1. Paul was troubled by the idols in Athens. Can an idol be something other than a figure of wood or stone?

2. How did Paul begin his talk to the Greeks and how did he end it? What is the one message we should take to the world? (Read Romans 10:9)

IN THE NAME OF THE LORD

Paul went away from Athens after this, and came to Corinth.

He found a Jew named Aquila. He was a man who was born in Pontus. He came from Italy with Priscilla, his wife, because Claudius ordered all the Jews to leave Rome.

Paul went to see them, and he stayed with them, because he did the same kind of work that they did. All of them made tents.

Paul spoke in the synagogue every Sabbath day and tried to convince the Jews and the Greeks.

After Silas and Timothy came from Macedonia, Paul spent all of his time preaching the gospel and telling the Jews that Jesus was the Christ.

But when they opposed him and spoke evil things against him, Paul shook his clothes as a sign against them, and said to them, "Your blood will be on your own heads. My responsibility has ended. I will go to the Gentiles now." He went away from there and went into the house of a man named Titus Justus. He was a man who worshiped God, and his house was next to the synagogue. Crispus, the ruler of the synagogue, and all the people in his family believed in the Lord. Many of the Corinthians who heard also believed and were baptized.

The Lord said to Paul in a vision one night, "Do not be afraid. Speak and do not be quiet, because I am with you. No one will attack you or harm you, because I have many people in this city."

Paul lived there for one and a half years and taught God's Word to them.

When Gallio was the ruler of Achaia, the Jews came together against Paul and took him to court and said, "This man tries to convince people to worship God in a way that is against the law."

But when Paul was about to speak, Gallio said to the Jews, "Jews, there would be a reason for me to listen to you, if something wrong or evil had been done. But settle it among yourselves if these are things about words and names and your law, because I will not be a judge of these things." Then he made them go out of the court. All of them took Sosthenes, the ruler of the synagogue, and beat him in front of the court, but Gallio did not give any attention to it.

Paul stayed there for many days after this. Then he went away from the brothers and sailed to Syria with Priscilla and Aquila. He cut off his hair in Cenchrea, because he had made a vow.

They came to Ephesus and Paul left them there. He went into the synagogue and talked with the Jews. They asked him to stay for a longer time, but he would not stay. But as he was about to go away, he said, "I will come to you again if God allows it." Then he sailed away from Ephesus.

After he came to Caesarea, Paul went up to greet the people of the church. Then he went down to Antioch, and stayed there for some time. He went through the area of Galatia and Phrygia after that, and gave strength to the believers.

There was a Jew named Apollos who was born in Alexandria. He was an educated man who came to Ephesus. He had much knowledge about the Word of God, and had been taught about the Lord's way. He had a strong spirit, and he spoke and taught with truth about the things of Jesus, although he only knew John's baptism. He began to speak without fear in the synagogue. But when Priscilla and Aquila heard him, they took him privately and explained God's way to him more completely.

The brothers encouraged Apollos when he wanted to go to

Achaia, and they wrote to the believers there and told them to welcome him. After he came there, he greatly helped the people who had become believers by God's grace. This is because he publicly proved in a powerful way that the Jews were wrong, and showed from what is written in the Word of God that Jesus was the Christ.

Acts 18:1-28

The first Christians understood that God was guiding their lives. Paul told the Jews in Ephesus that he would come to them again "if God allows it." James, the brother of Jesus, taught about this important truth many years later in his letter to the Christians:

"Now listen, you people who say, 'Today or tomorrow, we will go into a certain city and stay there a year and do business so we can get more money.' But you do not know what will happen in your life tomorrow. What is your life? You are like a cloud that is seen only for a short time and then disappears. So because of this, you should say, 'We will live and do this thing or that thing, if the Lord allows it.'"

James 4:13-15

DISCUSSION SUGGESTIONS:

1. When the Lord appeared to Paul in a vision, what did He say to him?

2. When Paul left the Ephesians, what did he say would decide whether he came again or not? What should guide our decisions and actions? (Read Psalm 32:8 and John 16:13)

REVERENCE FOR HIS NAME

Paul went through the middle part of the country while Apollos was at Corinth. Paul came to Ephesus and found some of the followers there.

He said to them, "Did you receive the Holy Spirit when you became believers?"

They said to him, "No, we have not even heard that there is a Holy Spirit."

He said, "What kind of baptism did you receive?" They said, "John's baptism."

Then Paul said, "John's baptism meant that you repented. John told the people they should believe in the One who would come later, and that One is Jesus."

So when they heard this, they were baptized in the name of the Lord Jesus.

When Paul laid his hands on them, the Holy Spirit came to them, and they spoke in other languages and prophesied. There were about twelve men in this group.

Then Paul went into the synagogue and spoke there for three months without fear. He talked to them and convinced them about the kingdom of God.

But some of them did not care about these things in their hearts, and they would not obey, and they said evil things about the Way to the people in the crowd.

So Paul went away from them. He took the believers with him, and he taught in the school of Tyrannus every day. This continued for two years, so all the people who lived in Asia, both the Jews and the Greeks, heard the Lord's message.

God did special and powerful miracles through Paul, and even pieces of cloth or clothes that had touched Paul were brought to the sick people, and the diseases left them, and evil spirits went out from them.

But there were some Jews who travelled to many places and ordered out evil spirits. They began to use the name of the Lord Jesus over the people who had evil spirits.

They said, "I order you to come out in the name of Jesus, whom Paul preaches about." There were seven sons of a chief priest, named Sceva, who did this. The evil spirit answered them, "I know Jesus and I know about Paul, but who are you?" The man who had the evil spirit jumped on them and beat all of them. They ran out of that house without their clothes, and with wounds on their bodies.

All the Jews and Greeks in Ephesus heard about this, and all of them became filled with fear, and the Lord Jesus Christ was being praised. Many of the people who had believed also came to admit and tell about the evil things they had done.

Many of the people who did strange magic brought their books together and burned them in front of everyone. They counted the price of the books, and it was fifty thousand pieces of silver. So the Lord's message continued to go out to many places, and became stronger in this powerful way.

Acts 19:1-20

When the first Christians preached the gospel of Jesus Christ, God proved their message was true with great works of power and miracles. The sick were healed when pieces of Paul's clothing touched them. These were unusual miracles, but God used them to confirm the message the first Christians preached. Paul talked about this to the Thessalonians in his first letter to them:

> *"Our gospel did not come to you in words only, but also with power and the Holy Spirit, and with great assurance of its truth. You know what kind of men we were when we lived among you. We did this because of you."*
>
> *1 Thessalonians 1:5*

DISCUSSION SUGGESTIONS:

1. After the Ephesians were baptized in the name of Jesus, what happened when Paul laid hands on them?

2. What were some of the special miracles that happened through Paul? What is the most important reason for signs and miracles? (Read John 20:30-31)

LOVING FALSE GODS

After all these things had ended, Paul decided to go to Jerusalem, and to go through Macedonia and Achaia on the way.

He said, "After I have been there, I must also go to Rome."

He sent two of his helpers, Timothy and Erastus, to Macedonia, but he stayed in Asia for a while.

A lot of trouble started about the Way at that time.

There was a man named Demetrius, who made things with silver. He made small silver temples of the goddess, Artemis, and he brought much business to the workers.

He called together the men who did the same kind of work, and said, "Men, you know we receive a large amount of money from this business. But you see and hear that Paul has convinced and turned away many people, not just here at Ephesus, but almost everywhere in Asia. Paul said that gods made by people's hands are not gods. There is a danger that people will not respect our business any longer, and also that people will think that the temple of the great goddess, Artemis, is not important. Also, the greatness of the goddess, whom all Asia and the world worships, could even be taken away."

They were full of anger when they heard this, and they called out, "Artemis of the Ephesians is great!"

The city was filled with trouble, and all of them rushed together into the large meeting place and took the Macedonian men, Gaius and Aristarchus, who traveled with Paul.

The believers would not let Paul go into the large crowd of people when he wanted to. Some of the leaders of Asia who were his friends sent a message to him and begged him not to go into the large meeting place.

Some of the people in the meeting called out one thing, but other people called out different things, because the meeting was in great confusion. Most of the people did not know why they had come together there.

The Jews pushed Alexander to the front, and some of the people in the crowd called out to him to tell him what to do. Alexander made a sign with his hand, and wanted to defend himself in front of the people. But when they saw he was a Jew, all of them called out together for about two hours, "Artemis of the Ephesians is great!"

Then the officer from the city caused the crowd to be quiet, and he said, "Men of Ephesus, doesn't everyone know that the city of Ephesus is where the temple of the great Artemis is kept, and also her image that fell down from heaven? These are true facts, so you should be quiet and you should not do anything without thinking carefully first. You have brought these men here, but they are not thieves of the temple, and they did not say evil things about our goddess. The courts are open, and there are judges, so if Demetrius and the workers with him have something against any person, let them speak against each other. But if you want to say anything more about other kinds of matters, they must be settled in a regular law meeting. It is certain that there is a danger that we will be in trouble because of the violence that happened today, because there was not any reason for it, and we would not be able to give a reason for it." He ended the meeting after he spoke.

Paul sent for the believers after the trouble stopped. He encouraged them, and then left them and went to Macedonia.

He went through the places in that area and said many things to the people to encourage them.

He came into Greece after that, and stayed there for three months.

When it was time for him to sail to Syria, the Jews made a plan against him, so he decided to return through Macedonia. Sopater from Berea, who was Pyrrhus's son, Aristarchus and Secundus from Thessalonica, Gaius and Timothy from Derbe, and Tychicus and Trophimus from Asia went with Paul. But these men went ahead and waited for us at Troas.

Acts 19:21-20:5

There is only one true God. The first Christians preached this truth in a world that worshiped many false gods. Paul explained this in his first letter to the Corinthians:

"So, about eating food sacrificed to idols, we know that an idol has no meaning in the world, and that there is only one God. Even if there are people who are called gods, whether in heaven or on earth (and it is true that there are many gods and many lords), but for us, there is only one God, the Father. All things came from Him, and we live for Him, and there is only one Lord, Jesus Christ, through whom all things came, and we live because of Him."

1 Corinthians 8:4-6

DISCUSSION SUGGESTIONS:

1. Do you think Demetrius the silversmith had more than one 'idol?'

2. What things could become 'idols' for people today? What must we remember about this? (Read Exodus 20:3 and Mark 12:28-30)

MORE JOY IN GIVING

We sailed away from Philippi after the Feast of the Unleavened Bread, and met those men in Troas five days after that. Then we stayed there for seven days.

We met together to break bread on the first day of the week. Paul talked with the people because he had decided to leave the next day, and he continued his message until twelve o'clock that night. There were many lamps in the room at the top of the house where we met together.

A young man named Eutychus sat in a window and was becoming very sleepy. As Paul continued to talk longer, Eutychus became completely asleep and fell down from the third floor. He was dead when they lifted him up.

Paul went down to him and threw himself on him, and put his arms around him and said, "Do not be troubled, because he is alive."

Then Paul went up again and broke the bread and ate. He talked with them for a long time, until early the next morning. Then he went away.

The people brought the young man home, and he was alive. They were very comforted.

But we went ahead of Paul to the ship and sailed to Assos, where Paul would join us on the ship. Paul chose this plan because he wanted to go there on land. We took him onto the ship when he met us at Assos, and then we went to Mitylene.

We sailed from there and came to the place near Chios the next day. We went to Samos on the day after that, and then we came to Miletus the next day. Paul had decided to sail past Ephesus, so he would not have to stay for a long time in Asia.

Paul did this because he was trying to go quickly, so he could be in Jerusalem, if possible, on the Day of Pentecost.

Paul sent a message to Ephesus from Miletus and asked the leaders of the church to come to him.

When they came to him, he said to them, "You know how I lived all the time when I was with you, since the first day I came to Asia. I served the Lord in a humble way, and with many tears, and during troubles that came to me because of the evil plans of the Jews. I did not stop preaching to you about anything that would help you. I taught you publicly and in people's houses, and I strongly told the Jews and Greeks that they must repent and turn to God, and have faith in our Lord Jesus. I must go to Jerusalem now, because the Spirit told me to go. I do not know the things that will happen to me there. I only know that in every city the Holy Spirit tells me strongly that prisons and troubles are waiting for me. But my life is not important to me, if only I can complete my purpose, and the work that I received from the Lord Jesus, to tell about the gospel of God's grace. Now I know that none of you, among whom I went and preached about the kingdom, will see me any more. So I tell you this day that I am not guilty of the blood of any person, because I did not stop myself from preaching to you the complete purpose of God. Give attention to yourselves, and all of the group of believers of whom the Holy Spirit has made you leaders, so you can be shepherds of the Lord's church that He bought with His own blood. I know that some men who are like wild wolves will come among you when I go away, and they will try to destroy the flock. Men will come even from among your group to change the truth, and they will cause Christ's followers to follow them. So be careful and remember that I never stopped warning each of you about this, night and day, with tears, for three years. Now I give you to God and to the message about His grace. It is able to build you up and allow you to have the inheritance God has for all the people who are made holy. I did not desire any person's silver, gold or clothes. You know that I have worked with my own hands to give myself the things I need, and also to give the people who were with me what they needed. I showed you by everything I did that you must help the people who are weak by working hard in this way, and remember the words of the Lord Jesus, 'There is more joy in giving than in receiving.'"

Paul went down on his knees, and prayed with all of them after he spoke.

All of them cried and put their arms around Paul's neck and kissed him. The thing that made them very sad was that he said they would not see him again.

Then they went with him to the ship.

Acts 20:6-38

Paul told the leaders in the church at Ephesus that he knew prison and troubles were waiting for him, but what was important was to complete his purpose of preaching the gospel of God's grace. The apostle Peter talked about this in his first letter:

"Dear friends, don't be surprised at the troubles that are among you. They have come to test you, as though a strange thing is happening to you. But have joy because you are sharing in Christ's suffering, so you can be full of great joy when His glory

is shown. You are blessed if you have evil spoken against you because of Christ's name, because the spirit of glory and of God is with you. Be sure that none of you suffer because you killed another person, did evil things or caused trouble in other people's lives. But you should not feel shame if you suffer because you are a Christian, but give glory to God because of that name."

1 Peter 4:12-16

DISCUSSION SUGGESTIONS:

1. Was Paul worried or frightened about what might be waiting for him when he left Ephesus? What did Paul say was most important to him?

2. Do Christians today need to worry about what will happen? (Read Psalm 27:1 and 1 Peter 5:7)

THE WILL OF THE LORD

We went away from them after that, and sailed directly to Cos. We came to Rhodes the next day, and went to Patara from there.

We found a ship that was going to Phoenicia and we went on it and began to sail. When we saw Cyprus, we went to the south of it, and sailed to Syria. We came to Tyre, because everything had to be taken off the ship there.

We found the followers and stayed there for seven days. They told Paul through the Spirit that he should not go to Jerusalem.

We continued on our trip after our time there had ended, and all of them, with their wives and children, came with us until we were outside the city. Then we went down on our knees on the shore and prayed. We said good-by to each other after that, and we went on the ship, and they returned home.

We came to Ptolemais after our trip to Tyre. We greeted the brothers there and stayed with them for one day. We went away the next day, and came to Caesarea.

We went into the house of Philip, who was a preacher of the gospel. He was one of the Seven, and we stayed with him. He had four daughters who were not married and they were prophetesses.

We stayed there for several days, and a prophet named Agabus came down from Judea. He came to us and took Paul's belt, and tied his own hands and feet with it.

He said, "The Holy Spirit says that in this way the Jews at Jerusalem will tie up the man who owns this belt, and they will give him to the Gentiles." All of us and the people who lived in that city begged Paul not to go to Jerusalem when we heard that.

Then Paul answered, "Why do you cry and cause my heart to be sad? I am ready to have chains put on my body, and also to die in Jerusalem for the name of the Lord Jesus."

When we knew that we could not convince him, we stopped, and we said, "Let the will of the Lord be done."

Acts 21:1-14

The apostle Paul knew that part of God's will for his life involved trials and persecution. He explained this in his first letter to the Thessalonian Christians:

"We sent Timothy, our brother and God's servant in the gospel of Christ, to make you strong and to encourage you in your faith, so no one would turn away from their faith by these troubles. You know that we have been chosen for these troubles, because we told you when we were with you that we were going to suffer trouble, and you know well that it happened. This was why I sent Timothy to you, when I could not endure it any longer, so I could know about your faith. I was afraid the tempter had tempted you, and our work would be useless."

1 Thessalonians 3:2-5

DISCUSSION SUGGESTIONS:

1. What sign did the prophet Agabus use to show that there were trials ahead for Paul?

2. What did Paul say when his friends begged him not to go to Jerusalem? What must we always be ready to say? (Read Matthew 6:9-10 and Luke 22:42)

Persevering Through Trouble

We made ourselves ready after this, and went up to Jerusalem. Some of the followers from Caesarea also went with us. They brought us to a man named Mnason, who was from Cyprus. He was one of the first followers of Christ, and we were going to stay with him.

The brothers welcomed us with joy when we came to Jerusalem. Paul and all of us went to see James the next day, and all the leaders were there. After Paul had greeted them, he told them everything God had done among the Gentiles through his work. They praised God when they heard it.

They said to him, "You see, brother, many thousands of Jews have become believers, and they all have great desire to obey the laws. They were told that you teach all the Jews who live among the Gentiles to turn away from Moses, and that you tell them not to circumcise their children, or follow the traditions. Then what should we do? They will certainly hear that you have come. So do what we tell you. We have four men here who have made a vow. Take these men and make yourself pure along with them and give them the money they need so they can cut off their hair. Then everyone will know that the things they were told about you are not true, and that you also live in the right way and obey the laws. We wrote to the Gentile believers and told them about our decision that they should not eat food that is offered to idols, blood, and meat from animals that are strangled, and that they should keep themselves away from sexual sin."

The next day Paul took the men, and he made himself pure, along with them. Then he went into the temple, to tell them when the time to be made pure would end, and when the offering would be given for each one of them.

When the seven days had almost ended, the Jews from Asia saw Paul in the temple. They caused trouble to start among the people in the crowd and they put their hands on him, and called out, "People of Israel, help! This is the man who preaches to all people everywhere against our people, our laws, and this place. He also brought Greeks into the temple and has made this holy place impure."

They said this because they saw Trophimus, the Ephesian, with Paul in the city, and they thought Paul had brought him into the temple. Everyone in the city was troubled, and the people ran together and took Paul, and pulled him out of the temple. The doors were shut immediately.

While the people were trying to kill Paul, news came to the chief captain of the soldiers that there was trouble and confusion in all of Jerusalem. He immediately took the soldiers and captains and ran down to the crowd. The people stopped beating Paul when they saw the chief captain and the soldiers.

Then the chief captain came and took Paul and ordered his men to tie him up with two chains. He asked who he was, and what he had done. Some of the people in the crowd shouted one thing, but other people shouted different things. The chief captain could not get the truth because there was too much noise, so he ordered his men to bring Paul into the army building.

The soldiers had to carry Paul when he came to the stairs because the people in the crowd were very violent. The crowd of people followed them and called out, "Kill him!"

Acts 21:15-36

When Christians suffer or are persecuted, God helps them to stand firm. Paul encouraged the Philippian Christians to do this:

> *"But your way of life should be like the gospel of Christ says it should be. So I will know that you remain strong, in one spirit, and with one mind, working for the faith of the gospel, whether I come and see you, or am away from you. Do not fear in any way the people who oppose you. This is a sign to them that they will be destroyed, and it is a sign to you that God will save you. It is given to you because of Christ, not only to believe in Him, but also to suffer for Him, because you have the same problems that you saw me have, and that you hear I still have."*
>
> *Philippians 1:27-30*

DISCUSSION SUGGESTIONS:

1. What happened to Paul that was foretold by Agabus in Caesarea?

2. Could Paul have decided not to go to Jerusalem? What made Paul strong and what should we remember about facing troubles? (Read John 16:33)

GOD'S PURSUING LOVE

As he was going to be brought into the temple, Paul said to the chief captain, "Can I say something to you?"

He said, "Do you speak Greek? Aren't you the Egyptian who started a rebellion, and led four thousand killers into the wilderness some time ago?"

Paul said, "I am a Jew from Tarsus, in Cilicia, so I am a member of an important city. I beg you, please let me speak to the people."

The captain allowed him to speak, and Paul stood on the stairs and made a sign to the people with his hand.

When everything had become very quiet, he spoke to them in the Hebrew language.

Paul said, "Brothers and fathers, listen to my defense."

They became even more quiet when they heard him speak to them in the Hebrew language.

Paul said, "I am a Jew and I was born in Tarsus, in Cilicia, but I was brought up in this city. I was a student of Gamaliel and I was taught completely the law of our fathers. I had a great desire for God, just like all of you who are here today. I persecuted the people from this Way until they died, and I put chains on both men and women, and put them into prisons. The high priest and the group of leaders can prove that it is true, because I received letters from them to give to their brothers in Damascus. I even traveled to Damascus to put chains on those people who were there, and to bring them to Jerusalem to be punished. I went on my way and came near to Damascus in the middle of the day. Suddenly, a very bright light shined from heaven around me. I fell to the ground and heard a voice say to me, 'Saul, Saul, why do you persecute me?' I answered, 'Lord, who are you?' He said to me, 'I am Jesus of Nazareth, whom you persecute.' The people who were with me saw the light, but they did not understand the voice of the person who spoke to me. Then I said, 'Lord, what should I do?' The Lord said to me, 'Get up and go to Damascus, and you will be told there about the things that have been chosen for you to do.' I could not see because of the brightness of that light, so the people who were with me took my hand and led me, and I came into Damascus. There was a man named Ananias who was faithful to the law, and the Jews there respected him. He came to me and stood near me and said 'Brother Saul, receive your sight.' I looked up and saw him at that moment. He said, 'The God of our fathers has chosen you to know His will, to see the Righteous One, and to hear words from His mouth, because you will tell all people about Him because of what you have seen and heard. So what are you waiting for now? Get up and be baptized, and wash away your sins by calling on His name.' While I was praying in the temple after I returned to Jerusalem, I saw a vision. I saw the Lord say to me, 'Make yourself ready and go out from Jerusalem quickly, because they will not accept what you say about Me.' I said, 'Lord, they know I went to all the synagogues and put in prison and beat the people who believe in You. I also stood near when Stephen, the man who was telling people about You, was killed. I showed that I agreed, because I guarded the coats of the people who killed him.' He said to me, 'Go, because I will send you far away to the Gentiles.'"

The people listened to Paul until he said this, and then they began to shout and said, "Take away this man from the earth, because it is not right for him to live!"

They shouted, and threw off their coats from their bodies, and threw dust into the air.

The chief captain ordered his men to bring Paul into the army building, and he said that Paul should be beaten and questioned, so he could know why the people shouted against him in that way.

As they put him in the right position to beat him, Paul said to the captain who stood near there, "Is it lawful for you to beat a man who is a Roman, and who has not been judged guilty?"

The captain went to the chief captain when he heard that, and told him what Paul said. Then the captain said, "What are you going to do? This man is a Roman."

The chief captain came and said to Paul "Tell me, are you a Roman?" He said, "Yes." The chief captain answered, "I paid a large amount of money to become a Roman." Paul said, "I was born a Roman."

Those who were going to ask him questions stood away from him immediately. The chief captain was afraid when he knew Paul was a Roman, and also because he had put chains on him.

Acts 21:37-22:29

When God's love reached the apostle Paul, he was completely changed! Once he realized what Christ's death meant for him, he could no longer live for himself. He told about this in his second letter to the Corinthian Christians:

"Christ's love controls us, because we are convinced that one man died for all people, and so, all people have died. He died for all people, so the people who live should not live for themselves any longer, but for Him, who died and who was

brought back to life again for them. So from this time forward, we do not think about anyone the way a natural person does. We thought about Christ the way a natural person does at one time, but we do not know Him in this way any longer. So a person is completely new if he is united with Christ. Old things have gone away, and the new things have come."

2 Corinthians 5:14-17

Discussion Suggestions:

1. What kind of person was Paul before he went to Damascus?

2. What changed Paul and what did Paul do that showed he was changed? What is it that makes people new? (Read Romans 6:3-4)

GOD IS IN CONTROL

But the chief captain wanted to know for sure why the Jews spoke against Paul, so the next day he took Paul's chains off, and ordered the chief priests and all the Council to come together. Then he brought Paul and put him in front of them.

Paul looked straight at the Council and said, "Brothers, I have lived in the presence of God in a way that is right and good, even until this day."

The high priest, Ananias, ordered the men who stood near him to hit his mouth.

Then Paul said to him, "God will hit you, because you are like a dirty wall that is painted white. You sit here and judge me by the law, but you go against the law and hit me!"

The men who stood near there said, "Do you speak evil against God's high priest?" Paul said, "Brothers, I did not know he was the high priest, because it is written, 'Do not speak evil against a ruler of your people.'"

But Paul saw that one part of the group was the Sadducees and the other part was the Pharisees, so he called out in the council, "Brothers, I am a Pharisee, and a son of Pharisees. I am being judged because of my hope that dead people will be brought back to life from death."

A disagreement began between the Pharisees and Sadducees when Paul said that, and the group was divided. They were divided because the Sadducees did not believe in angels or spirits or in people coming back to life from death, but the Pharisees believed in all of these things.

So a great noise started, and some of the teachers of the law who were Pharisees stood and argued strongly, "We do not find anything evil in this man. Maybe a spirit or an angel really spoke to him."

A great disagreement started, and the chief captain was afraid they would tear Paul into pieces. So he ordered the soldiers to go down and take Paul away from them by force, and bring him into the army building.

The Lord stood near Paul the next night, and said, "Have courage, because in the same way you have told people about Me in Jerusalem, so you must also tell people about Me in Rome."

The Jews came together the next morning, and made an oath to themselves that they would not eat or drink anything until they had killed Paul. There were more than forty of them who were a part of this secret plan.

They came to the chief priests and the leaders, and said, "We have made a serious oath to ourselves not to taste anything until we have killed Paul. So you and the Council should tell the chief captain to bring him down to you as though you want more information to judge these things about him. We will be ready to kill him even before he comes here."

But the son of Paul's sister heard about their evil plan, and he came into the army building to tell Paul.

Paul asked one of the captains to come to him, and said, "Take this young man to the chief captain, because he has something to tell him."

So he took him to the chief captain and said, "Paul, the prisoner, called me to him, and asked me to bring this young man to you, because he has something to tell you."

So the chief captain took his hand, and led him away and asked him privately, "What is it that you want to tell me?"

He said, "The Jews have agreed to ask you to bring Paul down tomorrow to the Council, as though they want to ask more questions about him. Do not listen to them, because there are forty men who are waiting to attack Paul. They have made an oath to themselves not to eat or drink anything until they have killed him. They are ready now, and they are waiting for you to agree to do what they will ask you." So the chief captain let the young man go, and ordered him, "Do not tell anyone that you have told me these things."

The chief captain called two of the captains to him and said, "Make ready two hundred soldiers, seventy men on horses, and two hundred men with spears, to go to Caesarea. Be ready tonight at about nine o'clock." He also told them to get horses to put Paul on, and to bring him safely to Felix, the ruler.

Then he wrote this letter, "Most excellent ruler, Felix, I, Claudius Lysias, greet you. The Jews took this man and were going to kill him soon, but I came to them with soldiers and saved him, after I learned that he was a Roman. I brought him down to their Council because I wanted to know why they accused him. I learned that they accused him because of questions about their laws. But he was not accused of anything that deserves death or prison. I sent him to you when I was told that there was an evil plan against this man. I also ordered the men who accused him to tell you why they are accusing him."

So the soldiers did what they were ordered to do. They took Paul and brought him to Antipatris during the night. But they left the next day and returned to the army building, while the men on horses went on with Paul. The men on horses came to Caesarea, and they gave the letter to the ruler, and they also gave Paul to him.

After he read the letter, he asked what area Paul came from, and learned that he was from Cilicia.

The ruler said, "I will listen to you when the men who are accusing you come here." Then he ordered his men to guard Paul in Herod's palace.

Acts 22:30-23:35

The apostle Paul knew that no matter what happened to him, God was always working in everything for his good. He explained why in his letter to the Romans:

"We know God causes all things to work together for good for the people who love Him and who are called by Him for His purpose. He chose the people He knew before to be changed to be like His Son, so His Son would be first among many brothers. He also called the people whom He chose, and He made them right with himself. He also glorified the people whom He made right with himself. So what will we say about these things? Who is against us if God is for us?"

Romans 8:28-31

DISCUSSION SUGGESTIONS:

1. What did Paul say he and the other Pharisees believed that the Sadducees were judging him about?

2. What did the Lord tell Paul would happen as a result of Paul's arrest? What does this teach us about God's ways?" (Read Psalm 37:23-25)

SPEAKING BEFORE RULERS

Five days after that Ananias, the high priest, came with some leaders and with Tertullus, an expert in the Law. They spoke to the ruler against Paul.

When Paul was brought in, Tertullus began to speak against him, and he said to the ruler, "We have experienced great peace because of you, and your wisdom has brought many good changes in this nation. Most excellent Felix, we accept this with great thanks, in every way and everywhere. But I do not want to trouble you any longer, so I beg you to be kind and listen to a few words that we want to say to you. We have seen that this man causes trouble and starts rebellions among the Jews, everywhere in the world. He is a leader of a religious group named the Nazarenes. He also tried to make the temple impure. So we took him by force. But Lysias, the chief captain, came and took him from us with great violence. You can ask him questions, and you will be able to learn about all these things we speak against him."

The other Jews also joined them to speak against Paul, and said that these things were true.

The ruler made a sign to Paul to speak, so Paul answered, "I know you have been a judge to this nation for many years, so I make my defense with joy, because you know I went up to Jerusalem to worship not more than twelve days ago. They did not find me arguing with anyone in the temple or causing trouble to begin among the people in the crowd, either in the synagogue or in the city. They also cannot prove to you the things they now speak against me. But I admit to you I serve the God of our fathers in the Way that they call a false religious group. I believe all the things that agree with the laws and all the things that are written in the books of the prophets. I have hope in God, just like these men have, that both the righteous and unrighteous people will be brought back to life from death. This is why I try very hard always to have a conscience that is free, by not doing wrong things to God or people. I came to my nation to bring gifts for the people who are poor and to give offerings, after being away for several years. They found me in the temple doing this, and I had been made pure in the temple and there was not any crowd or any trouble. But there are some Jews from Asia who should be here in front of you to accuse me, if they have anything against me. Or these men here should say what wrong things they found in me when I stood in the presence of the Council, except for this one thing that I called out as I stood among them, 'It is about people being brought back to life from death that I am judged in your presence today.'"

But Felix, who had knowledge about the Way, stopped the meeting and said, "I will decide these things about you when Lysias, the chief captain, comes."

He gave orders to the captain that his men should continue to guard Paul, but that he should have some freedom, and his friends should be allowed to do things for him that he needed.

Several days after that, Felix came with Drusilla, his wife, who was a Jewish woman. He sent for Paul and listened to him speak about faith in Jesus Christ. Felix became afraid when Paul talked about righteousness, self-control and the judgment that will come later.

He said, "Go away now, but I will send for you when I have time."

He also hoped Paul would give him money, so he often sent for him and talked with him.

Two years after that, Porcius Festus became the ruler instead of Felix, and because Felix wanted to do a favor for the Jews, he kept Paul in prison.

Acts 24:1-27

Felix was like many people. He wanted to respond to God's message in his own time. Paul told the Corinthian Christians in his second letter that the time to receive Him is now:

"So we are sent to speak for Christ, as if God were calling people to Him through us. We urge you, as people who speak for Christ, to be brought together with God again. The One who did not have any sin, was made sin for us, so we could become the righteousness of God when we are united with Him. We urge you, as workers together with God, who have received God's grace, to not let it be wasted, because He says, 'I listened to you at the right time, and I helped you on the day of salvation.' Now is the right time. Now is the time of salvation."

2 Corinthians 5:20-6:2

DISCUSSION SUGGESTIONS:

1. What did Paul talk about that made Felix become afraid?

2. As he sent Paul away, when did Felix say he would listen to Paul and do people say the same thing today? What did Jesus say about this? (Read Mark 13:33-37)

PAUL BEFORE THE KING

Festus went up to Jerusalem from Caesarea, three days after he had come into the province. The chief priests and the leaders of the Jews told him the things they had against Paul, and they asked him strongly for a favor. They wanted him to send Paul to Jerusalem, because they were making a plan to kill him on the way. Festus answered that Paul was being guarded at Caesarea, and that he himself was going there soon.

He said, "Let those people who are your leaders go with me. Let them speak against him if he has done anything wrong."

After he had stayed with them for about eight or ten days, Festus went down to Caesarea. He sat in the judge's seat the next day, and ordered men to bring Paul to him.

The Jews from Jerusalem stood near Paul as he came, and they accused him of many things that they could not prove.

Paul defended himself and said, "I did not do any wrong things against the law of the Jews, or against the temple, or against Caesar."

But Festus wanted to do a favor for the Jews, so he answered Paul, "Will you go up to Jerusalem and be judged for these things there in my presence?"

But Paul said, "I am standing in Caesar's court now. This is where I should be judged. You also know very well I have not done any wrong things to the Jews. But I am willing to die if I did anything wrong, or if I did anything that deserves death. But no one can give me to the Jews if the things they have accused me of doing are not true. I ask for Caesar to be my judge."

Festus talked with his council, and then he answered, "You have asked for Caesar to be your judge, so you will go to Caesar."

A few days after that, King Agrippa and Bernice came to Caesarea to greet Festus. They stayed there for many days, and Festus told the king all the things about Paul.

He said, "There is a man whom Felix put into prison and left him there. The chief priest and leaders accused him, and asked me to condemn him, when I was in Jerusalem. I answered them that it is not the tradition of the Romans to give anyone to the people who accuse him before the person who is accused can meet with the people who accuse him and have the opportunity to defend himself about the things they are accusing him of doing. So they came together, and I did not wait a long time, but I sat in the judge's seat the next day and ordered the men to bring this man to me. The men who accused him stood, but they did not accuse him of doing the evil things that I thought they would accuse him of doing. But they disagreed with him about several things in their religion, and about a dead man named Jesus, whom Paul said was alive. I did not know enough about these things to ask questions, so I asked him if he would go to Jerusalem and be judged about these things there. But Paul asked to be kept there so the Emperor could make a decision. So I ordered him to be kept there until I could send him to Caesar."

Then Agrippa said to Festus, "I also want to listen to the man." He answered, "You will hear him tomorrow."

Agrippa came with Bernice the next day. They came in a way that looked very important. They went into the court room with the chief captains and the men from the city who were leaders. Then Festus ordered the men to bring Paul in.

Festus said, "King Agrippa, and all people who are present with us here, you see this man. All the Jewish people have complained to me, both in Jerusalem and here, and they said strongly that he should not live any longer. But I found that he did not do anything that deserves death. He asked for the Emperor to be his judge, and I have decided to send him there. I do not have anything certain to write to the Emperor about him, so I have brought him to all of you. King Agrippa, I brought him especially to you, so I could have something to write, after you have asked him questions. I am doing this because it does not seem wise to me to send a prisoner and not to say what wrong things he has done."

Acts 25:1-27

The apostle Paul stood unafraid before the king because he knew that the Lord stood with him. He told Timothy about this in his second letter:

"No one supported me at my first defense. They all left me. But it should not be held against them. The Lord stood with me and gave me strength, so the message could be fully preached through me, and all the Gentiles can hear it. I was saved from the lion's mouth. The Lord will save me from every evil act, and will bring me safely to His heavenly kingdom. Glory should be given to Him forever. Amen."

2 Timothy 4:16-18

DISCUSSION SUGGESTIONS:

1. Why did the Jewish leaders want Festus to send Paul back to Jerusalem to be judged?

2. When Festus tried to give the Jews what they wanted, what did Paul say that stopped them? Who helped Paul know what to say when he faced the judge's court? (Read John 14:26)

A POWERFUL TESTIMONY

Agrippa said to Paul, "You are allowed to speak for yourself."

Then Paul reached out his hand and began to defend himself, "King Agrippa, I think I am blessed that I can defend myself in your presence today about all the things the Jews have accused me of doing, especially because you know well all the Jewish traditions and questions. So I beg you to listen to me patiently. All the Jews know the way I have lived my life since the time I was young, from the beginning of my life in my nation, and also in Jerusalem. They have known about me for a long time, and they can tell you, if they are willing, that I was a Pharisee. That is the most serious group of our religion. Now I stand here to be judged because of the hope God promised to our fathers. Our twelve tribes served God night and day with true hearts, and hoped to receive that promise. Oh King, it is because of this hope that the Jews accuse me. Why do you think it is not possible for God to bring people back to life from death? It is true that I also thought I should do many things to go against Jesus from Nazareth. This is what I did in Jerusalem. After I received authority from the chief priests, I put many believers in prisons. I strongly agreed with the decision when the believers were killed. I often punished them in all the synagogues, and I tried to force them to say evil things against Jesus. I was very angry with them and I persecuted them. I even went to cities outside my country to persecute them. I traveled to Damascus, and I had authority and orders from the chief priests. I saw a light from heaven at about noon, as I went on my way. It was brighter than the sun, and it shone around me and the men who traveled with me. All of us fell to the ground, and I heard a voice say to me in the Hebrew language, 'Saul, Saul, why do you persecute me? It is hard for you to kick against the thorns.' I said, 'Lord, who are you?' The Lord said, 'I am Jesus whom you persecute. But get up and stand on your feet. I have appeared to you because I have chosen you to be My servant and to tell people what you have seen, and what I will show to you. I will save you from your own people and from the Gentiles. I will send you to open their eyes, so they can turn away from darkness to light, and from the power of Satan to God, so they can receive forgiveness for their sins, and the inheritance that those people who are made holy by faith in me will have.'"

"So King Agrippa," said Paul, "I obeyed the vision from heaven. I preached to the people from Damascus, and then to the people in Jerusalem, and to the people everywhere in the country of Judea, and to the Gentiles, so they can repent and turn to God and do the kinds of things that prove they have repented. It was because of these things that the Jews took me when I was in the temple, and tried to kill me. But I have received help from God, from then until now, and so I stand here and tell about these things to both the people who are not great and to those who are great. I do not say anything except the things the prophets and Moses said would happen. They said the Christ must suffer, and be brought back to life from death. So then He would be the first person to preach light both to our people and to the Gentiles."

While Paul was defending himself in this way, Festus said with a loud voice, "Paul, your mind is not right! Your great learning has caused your mind not to be right."

But Paul said, "Most excellent Festus, my mind is right, and I speak words that are true and have the right meaning. The king also knows about these things and I can speak freely to him. I am sure he knows about these things, because they were not done in secret. King Agrippa, do you believe the prophets? I know you do."

Agrippa said to Paul, "Do you think you can convince me in this short time to become a Christian?"

Paul said, "I pray to God that whether it is a short time or a long time, that you and also all those who are listening to me today, will become what I have become, except for these chains."

The king, the ruler, Bernice, and all the people who sat with them, stood. They spoke to each other after they had gone from the room.

They said, "This man has not done anything that deserves death or prison."

Agrippa said to Festus, "This man could be freed, if he had not asked for Caesar to be his judge."

Acts 26:1-32

Paul was faithful to his heavenly vision. Without fear he gave a powerful testimony of God's purpose and grace in his life. In his second letter to his young friend Timothy he encouraged him to do the same:

"God did not give us a spirit of fear, but a spirit of power, love and self-control. So do not feel shame about the testimony of our Lord, or feel shame because of me, His prisoner. But suffer with me for the gospel, by the power of God. He saved us and called us to live a holy life, not because of what we have done, but because of His own purpose and grace. This grace was given to us in Jesus Christ before the beginning of time, but it has

been shown now by the appearing of our Savior, Christ Jesus who destroyed death, and showed us everlasting life through the gospel. I was chosen to be a preacher, an apostle, and a teacher of this gospel. This is why I suffer these things. But I do not feel shame, because I know the One whom I have believed, and I am convinced that He is able to keep safe what I have trusted Him with, until that day."

2 Timothy 1:7-12

DISCUSSION SUGGESTIONS:

1. What did King Agrippa say after he listened to Paul's testimony?

2. What did Paul say he prayed for the king and the others who heard Paul? How did Paul learn to speak so boldly and wisely to these powerful rulers? (Read 1 Corinthians 2:13 & 16)

FAITH IN GOD'S PROMISE

When it was decided that we should sail to Italy, they gave Paul and some other prisoners to a captain named Julius, who was in the Augustan Regiment. We went onto a ship that belonged to Adramyttium. It was going to sail soon to the places along the shore of Asia. Then we went out into the sea. Aristarchus, a Macedonian man from Thessalonica, was with us. We stopped at Sidon the next day. Julius was kind to Paul, and he allowed him to go to his friends, so they could give him some things he needed.

Then we went out into the sea from there, and we sailed close to Cyprus, because the winds were blowing against us. After we sailed on the sea by the shore of Cilicia and Pamphylia, we came to Myra, a city of Lycia. There the captain found a ship from Alexandria that was going to sail to Italy, and he put us on it.

We sailed slowly for many days, and we came to Cnidus, but we had much trouble. The winds did not allow us to continue, so we sailed close to Crete, along the sea shore of Salmone. We moved along it, but we had much trouble, and we came to a place named Fair Havens, near the city of Lasea. Much time was lost, and the trip was now dangerous because it was also after the Fast now.

So Paul warned them, "Men, I can see that we will have great trouble on the trip, and there will be much loss of the things on the ship, and the ship, and also of our lives."

But the army captain was convinced by the captain of the ship and the man who drove the ship, and not by the things Paul said.

The harbor there was not a good place to stay during the winter, so most of the men wanted to continue to sail from there, and to try to go to Phoenix, if possible, and stay there during the winter. Phoenix is a harbor in Crete and it faces the southwest and northwest. They thought they had received the kind of weather they wanted when the south wind blew gently. So they pulled up the anchor, and sailed close to the shore along Crete. But a very strong wind named the 'northeaster' came from the island after a short time.

The ship stopped and could not sail into the wind, so we stopped trying to go against the wind, and we let the ship go in the direction of the wind.

We were able to control the lifeboat after we sailed close to a small island named Cauda, but we had much trouble. They put ropes around the ship after they had lifted the lifeboat onto the ship. They were afraid they would be thrown onto the sandbars of Syrtis, so they let the sea anchor down, and let the ship go in the direction of the wind.

We were beaten violently by the storm, so the next day we began to throw off some things from the ship. They threw out the ship's equipment with their hands on the third day. We lost all hope that we would be saved, because the sun and stars did not shine for many days, and the storm continued.

The men had not eaten any food for a long time, so Paul stood among them and said, "Men, you should have listened to me and not sailed from Crete, and then this destruction and loss would not have happened to you. But now, I ask you strongly to keep your courage, because no person's life will be lost, but only the ship will be lost. Last night an angel from the God to whom I belong and whom I serve, stood near me and said, 'Paul, do not be afraid. You must stand in the presence of Caesar, and God has given to you all those who sail with you.' So men, continue to have courage, because I have faith in God that this will happen just like He told me. But we must be thrown onto the sandbars of an island."

Acts 27:1-26

The Apostle Paul knew that God was always working all things according to His will, and that he could depend on God's promises. Paul explained this to the Ephesian Christians:

"He made known to us in all His wisdom and understanding the mystery of His will, because it was His kind plan, that He planned through Christ. His plan will be completed when the time is right. This plan is to bring together all things that God made, everything in heaven and on earth, and Christ will be the authority over all of it. We also received an inheritance from Him. We were chosen by the purpose of the One who makes all things happen the way He planned, so we who had hoped in Christ first, could praise God's glory."

Ephesians 1:9-12

DISCUSSION SUGGESTIONS:

1. When the storm made the men on the ship give up hope, what did Paul tell them?

2. What made Paul so sure that none of them would lose their lives? What can we learn from this? (Read Psalm 91:14-15 & Hebrews 6:17-19)

Protected from Danger

The wind was still moving us along in the sea of Adria on the fourteenth night, and at about midnight, the workers on the ship thought that they were going to come near to land soon.

They threw a rope into the water with a weight on the end of it, and they learned that the water was one hundred and twenty feet deep. They did this again after a short time, and learned that the water was ninety feet deep. They dropped four anchors from the back end of the ship, because they were afraid we would be thrown against the rocks. Then they prayed for daylight to come.

The workers on the ship wanted to try to leave the ship, so they put the lifeboat into the sea, as if they were putting out anchors from the front end.

Paul said to the captain and to the soldiers, "You cannot be saved unless these men stay on the ship."

Then the soldiers cut away the ropes from the boat, and let it fall off from the ship.

Just before the sun came up, Paul urged all of them to eat some food and he said, "Today is the fourteenth day that you have waited to see what would happen, and you have not eaten anything. So I urge you to eat some food, because it will give you strength. None of you will lose even a hair from your head."

After he had said this, he took bread and thanked God for it in the presence of all of them. Then he broke it and ate it.

They were all encouraged and they also ate some food. There

were two hundred and seventy six of us on the ship.

After they had eaten enough, they threw the grain out into the sea, so the ship could carry less weight.

When the sun came up, they did not know what place they were near, but they saw a bay with a shore, so they decided to sail the ship onto the shore. They threw off the anchors and left them in the sea, and at the same time they untied the ropes that held the rudder. Then they put up the front sail so the wind would blow the ship forward, and they went toward the shore.

But they came onto a sandbar and the ship stopped on the ground. The front end of the ship could not move, and the back end of it was broken into pieces, because the waves had hit it violently.

The soldiers planned to kill the prisoners, so none of them could swim away from the ship. But the captain did not allow them to do what they had planned, because he wanted to save Paul. He ordered the men who could swim to jump off the ship first and to go to the shore, and he told the other men to go by lying on top of boards or pieces of the ship. So in this way, all of them came to the shore safely.

After we were safe, we learned that the island was named Malta. The people who lived on the island were very kind to us. They started a fire and welcomed all of us, because it was raining and cold.

Paul put together some sticks, and as he put them on the fire, a snake came out because of the heat, and took hold of his hand.

When the people who lived on the island saw the snake hang from Paul's hand, they said to each other, "This man must be a killer. Although he was saved from the sea, justice will not let him live."

But Paul shook the snake off into the fire and he was not harmed. They expected him to become sick or fall down dead suddenly. But after they had waited for a long time and saw that nothing happened to him, they changed their thoughts and said he was a god.

There was a place near there that belonged to the chief leader of the island. His name was Publius. He welcomed us and was very kind to us and let us stay in his home for three days. His father was lying in bed and was suffering from fever and dysentery.

So Paul went to him and prayed. He laid his hands on the man and healed him. After this happened, the other people on the island who had diseases came and they were also healed.

They honored us in many ways, and when we were ready to sail away, they put the things we needed on the ship.

Acts 27:27-28:10

The apostle Paul knew that no matter what trials he faced, nothing could separate him from the love and care of Christ. He declared this in his letter to the Romans:

"Who will separate us from the love of Christ? Will trouble or persecution or not having food and clothes, or danger or even death? It is written, 'We are in danger of being killed at all times for you. We are like sheep that are going to be killed.' No, we have even more than victory in all these things, through Him who loved us. This is because I know and do not have any doubts that death, or life, or angels, or evil spirits, or things that are present, or things that will happen in the future, or powers, or things above, or things below, or anything that is made, will not be able to separate us from the love of God, that is in Christ Jesus our Lord."

Romans 8:35-39

DISCUSSION SUGGESTIONS:

1. What happened when Paul put sticks on the fire?

2. What did the people of Malta think would happen next and what did happen? What saying of Jesus did this fulfill? (Read Mark 16:15-18)

PREACHING IN PRISON

After three months, we began to sail in a ship that had stayed on the island during the winter. It was a ship from Alexandria, that had the sign 'The Twin Brothers' on the front.

We stopped at Syracuse and stayed there for three days. We sailed from there and came to Rhegium. There was a south wind the next day, and we came to Puteoli on the second day.

We found some brothers there, and they asked us to stay with them for seven days. Then we went to Rome.

Some brothers there in Rome heard that we were coming, and they came to The Market of Appius and The Three Inns to meet us. Paul thanked God and was encouraged when he saw them.

After we went into Rome, Paul was allowed to stay by himself with the soldier who guarded him. Paul called the leaders of the Jews together after three days.

After they had come together, he said, "Brothers, I was taken when I was in Jerusalem, and was given to the Romans, although I did not do anything against the people or against the traditions of our fathers. They wanted to free me after they asked me questions, because there was not any reason why I should be killed. But the Jews spoke against this, so I had to ask for Caesar to be my judge, but it is not because I had anything to say against my nation. So it is for this reason that I asked to see you and talk to you. It is because of the hope of Israel that I am tied with this chain."

They said to him, "We did not receive letters from Judea about you, and none of the brothers who came reported or said evil things about you. But we want to hear from you what you think about this religious group, because we know that it is spoken against in all places."

They chose a day for a meeting with him, and large numbers of people came to the place where he was staying.

He explained things to them by telling them about the kingdom of God, and he tried to convince them about Jesus. He did this from the law of Moses and the writings of the prophets, from morning until evening.

Some of them were convinced by what he said, but some of them did not believe it.

They did not agree among themselves, and they began to leave after Paul said this last statement, "The Holy Spirit spoke the truth to your fathers through Isaiah the prophet. He said: 'Go to these people and say, "You will continue to hear, but you will never understand. You will continue to see, but you will never understand." This is because in their heart these people do not really want to understand. Their ears almost cannot hear and they have closed their eyes, because if they did not, they would see with their eyes, they would hear with their ears, they would understand with their heart, and they would turn to Me again and I would heal them.' So I want you to know that this salvation from God has been sent to the Gentiles, and they will listen."

He stayed for two whole years in the house he rented for himself, and he welcomed everyone who came to him.

He preached about the kingdom of God, and taught about the Lord Jesus Christ freely and openly, and no one tried to stop him.

Acts 28:11-31

All through the book of Acts we have seen the power of the Holy Spirit at work in the lives of the new Christians. Everything we read in Acts proves the truth of Jesus' promise before He returned to heaven:

"... you will receive power when the Holy Spirit comes to you, and you will tell people about Me in Jerusalem, in all of Judea and Samaria, and even in the farthest places of the earth."

Acts 1:8

DISCUSSION SUGGESTIONS:

1. What did Paul use to convince the Jews that Jesus was God's Son and the Savior?

2. Who did Paul say had spoken through the prophet Isaiah and who gave Paul the ability to speak fearlessly at his trial? For how long was this promise of the Holy Spirit's help to last? (Read John 14:16-17)